Empathy
Theory and Application in Psychotherapy

Empathy

Theory and Application in Psychotherapy

Renuka Sharma

With an Introduction by
Karin Brown

Nalanda International
Los Angeles (USA)

DK PRINTWORLD
Publishers of Indian Traditions

Cataloging in Publication Data — DK

[Courtesy: D.K. Agencies (P) Ltd. <docinfo@dkagencies.com>]

Sharma, Renuka M.

Empathy : theory and application in psychotherapy / Renuka Sharma ; with an introduction by Karin Brown. — Rev. ed.

p. cm.

Includes bibliographical references (p.) and index.

ISBN 13: 9788124607299

1. Empathy. I. Title.

DDC 152.41 23

ISBN 13: 978-81-246-0729-9

First published in New York, in 1993
by The Edwin Press (Permission granted)

Second Edition published in India, in 2014

Published by:

Nalanda International

"Nalanda", 6418, Spring Park Avenue
Los Angeles, CA - 90056 (USA)
Phones: (310)-430-8057; *Fax*: (213)-341 0156
Web: www.nalandainternational.com

and

D.K. Printworld (P) Ltd.

Regd. office : *Vedaśrī*, F-395, Sudarshan Park
(Metro Station: Ramesh Nagar)
New Delhi - 110 015
Phones: (011) 2545 3975, 2546 6019; *Fax*: (011) 2546 5926
e-mail:indology@dkprintworld.com
Web: www.dkprintworld.com

Printed by: D.K. Printworld (P) Ltd., New Delhi

For
Tara Singh–Sharma, Chandra Pratap Sharma, and Devi Rasa

Preface
To the Second Edition

RENUKA Sharma passed away prematurely at age forty-four on October, 31st, 2002 in Melbourne, Australia, after struggling with a pernicious form of terminal cancer over a protracted period, part of which she also spent in temporary residence in the United States and as well as in India. She was in her prime, professionally and in personal life.

The present book, as she describes in her Preface to the original edition, arose in a more general way during her training in medicine and in psychiatry, but more specifically in her training in psychoanalysis and her practice as a feminist psychotherapist. More concretely, the pages of the book emerged from a felt need to expand on her earlier paper on "Empathy" which was published in the *Australian and New Zealand Journal of Psychiatry* in 1992 in tandem with her higher-studies work towards a Masters in Psychological Medicine (and later Ph.D. thesis on Emotions and Affectivity, which remained incomplete due to the onset of the irreversible health challenge).

The work was hailed by her peers as marking an original contribution, that set out admirably toward tackling the formidable array of problems posed by empathy in the philosophical, clinical and social domains; it was deemed that the work should become an important stimulus for debate and creative thinking to guide and clarify future explorations associated with the concept of empathy. Hence an effort was made towards the publication. The book has long been out of print, and not widely accessible.

In the tenth year marking Renuka's demise, as her surviving partner and intellectual companion, I undertook to re-issue the book. In this effort, I was assisted by a number of friends and colleagues. Karin Brown (my philosophy colleague from San Jose State University's Comparative Philosophy team) kindly agreed to write a new Introduction, not least from the point-of-view of updates from recent work in the area and some connections she sees between Renuka's thinking on empathy/compassion with phenomenology and feminist thought. Patrick Hutchings, Sherah Bloor, Peter Wong and Amy Rayner at the Sophia Projects office encouraged me to proceed with the task – especially after the powerful evocation that Patrick offered at the funeral services, cited in the obituary by Max Charlesworth – another source of inspiration to Renuka – that appeared in the "The Age" (Melbourne) 30.12.2002.

Beautiful face, mind heart
The dark/Shadow/
The wakening in brightness

Brightness, radiance, luminosity are the exact words for the spirit of Renuka Sharma, who continued to work on empathy, emotions, ethics, gender and justice even in the midst of frantic travelling and aggressive treatments.

Hazel Rowley (before her premature demise also in 2011), Tina M. Benson and Liza Lichtinger (Bay Area/SF-based Optimal Psychotherapists) read the first edition and gave me some helpful feedback. While Renuka's favourite Devi (of the canine kind) is also no more, her (Devi's) daughter Rasa is still in the care of their long-appointed nanny, Nina Ruhle. Together they exude and remind one irresistibly of the aura of empathy and much mirth that surrounded the Sharma–Bilimoria family-homes in Camberwell (Melbourne) and in

Venus Bay (Victorian seaside) during the days of intellectual and cultural creativity: a moment that has all but slipped away into the darkened mirror of her story.

Purushottama Bilimoria, Ph.D.
Chitravarthi River
Raishelama
September 2013

Preface
To the First Edition

THE aim of this study broadly speaking, is to arrive at a lucid – and as comprehensive as possible – understanding of the concept of empathy, especially in its theoretical and clinical frame of reference within the epistemé of psychoanalysis. Towards this end, a comprehensive literature search was undertaken with a view to situating the notion of empathy within the historical context of its origins and its subsequent conceptual development in psychoanalysis and psychotherapy.

In Chapter 1, a historical account of the origins and subsequent development of the notion is outlined. It traces the early roots of the English term "empathy" in Greek aesthetics and its German equivalence. The discussion shows, in very broad terms, how the term "empathy" is related to its wider usage in popular culture, in phenomenology, anthropology and related fields of study in the human sciences.

Chapter 2 explores problems with the various psychoanalytic definitions of the term. One consideration put forward is that the problems are due in large measure to inherent difficulties in defining the term and they are further accentuated by the language and polemics of the discourse of psychoanalysis. Chapter 3 deals with the major psychoanalytic contributions towards a definition of empathy. It surveys and presents a critique of the specific thinking and contributions of psychoanalytic writers from a wide spectrum – Freud and

Fliess through Kohut to Shapiro. Their specific understanding and therapeutic applications are considered with regard to aetiology, description, function and the epistemological status of empathy within the psychoanalytic framework. In the second part of this chapter empathy is analysed in relation to certain other important psychoanalytic and therapeutic framing concepts, in particular, countertransference, projective identification and introspection.

Chapter 4 brings together the previous discussions towards arriving at a reformulation of the concept of empathy in its clinical and epistemological trope within the broader context of social psychology and cognitive developmental studies. The chapter draws on examples from clinical studies. Further trajectories for research and clinical perspective are discussed in providing analogies towards understanding this uncompleted development of a most important and promising concept in the history of psychoanalysis.

The discussion Chapter 5 ends with an attempt to explore some implications of the process of empathic understanding in terms of the preceding phenomenological analysis and critique of the existing theory and practice.

Genesis of the Work and Acknowledgement

The idea of doing this work arose shortly after returning to Melbourne from a year's sabbatical in New York, most of which was spent reading widely in the areas of psychoanalysis and philosophy. My encounters and deep interchanges with researchers in these broad disciplinary and interdisciplinary fields inspired my interest towards looking at the issue of intersubjectivity a little more closely. One other inspiration came from conversations I had in Stony Brook with a number of colleagues, especially Prof. Ed Casey, Prof. Patrick Heelan, Prof. Richard Friedman and Prof. Richard Gard. Robert Magliola, also a visiting fellow in Stony Brook, pointed me towards a possible link between intersubjectivity and the Buddhist notion of compassion (*karuṇā*).

Shortly afterwards I attended a tenth anniversary conference marking Kohut's death in Chicago, where a breakfast conversation with Dr Bernard Brandchaft threw further light on Bion's efforts to articulate the phenomenon of the unknown and the dire attempt on the part of another to facilitate access to it. Then an A.K. Rice workshop on authority and leadership highlighted the problems in perceiving accurately individual motivations within group situations. This was followed by a series of seminars on contemporary interpersonal pscyhoanalysis taken by John Fiscalini at The William Alanson White Institute in New York, where the vast lacuna in the understanding of the interpersonal relations in therapeutic stance came to light. Sondra Wilk's generosity with time and resources provided further encouragement. An extended winter month spent in Setauket forest by the university in Stony Brook on Long Island helped crystallize the problem I had been grappling with. It is around then that I decided that the term "empathy", that had now become one of the mainstays of psychoanalysis/ psychotherapy, was in need of a thorough revisioning. Happily, Dr Joseph Lichtenberg with his colleagues had put out a two-volume collection of essays on empathy which provided much needed basic resources for my reflections to take a further step. In subsequent discussions and correspondences with Dr Lichtenberg – as also with Prof. Joseph Lichtenberg, Associate Prof. Sidney Bloch and Dr Peter Parker and Dr George Halasz – my ideas and the thesis I have worked towards began to take clearer form and shape. In subsequent seminars with the Australian Group Psychotherapy Programme and participation in a course on "Psychoanalytic Thinking" with Dr Stanley Gold and Dr Alasdair Bain, as well as discussions with Prof. Graeme Smith, I gained further structural insights into the problem at hand. Further encouragement arrived through the numerous positive feedback and requests for offprints I received for my article, "Empathy – A Retrospective on Its Development in Psychotherapy", in the *Australian and New Zealand Journal of Psychiatry* (September 1992, **26**(2): 377-90).

Although the present work pre-dates in thought my training in psychiatry, the actual writing occurred alongside my first two years of training in psychiatry. And so my developing thoughts on empathy were constantly tested by the numerous patients I cared for and interacted with in the institutional setting during long hours of work. These encounters, which called upon a deep sensitivity to *Sorge,* helped to lighten the therapeutic process while they also challenged the limits of the empathic resource.

Apart from the healthy academic and institutional inputs, numerous encounters and protracted conversations or "banter" with close friends and confidents fuelled my intuitions, which in turn broadened the hermeneutical horizons of my inquiry and deep feelings for the subject matter. In particular, I owe it to Smt Vishalakshi, Edie Kelvin, Anie Rosenthal and my partner, Purushottama Bilimoria.

Melbourne, Australia Renuka Sharma
May 1993

Foreword

Empathy is a term much used in popular and professional cultures. Its usage has acquired a wide range of meanings often contradictory when taken as a whole. This could reflect a number of semantic, epistemological and paradigmatic polemics which are obscured by overly descriptive accounts of the subjective experience. This study by Renuka Sharma provides a thorough and systematic "deconstruction" of the literature allowing for some clarification of the meta-theoretical schemata presently in use.

This book is a timely addition to the growing interest in the area of emotions both within the psychoanalytic and philosophical literatures. The discussions within both disciplines are legion and they centre around the issues of knowing another; authenticity; alterity; incommensurability; and a host of problems about subjectivity and perception. Perhaps erudite discussions aid in the therapist's task of maintaining an authentic stance towards meeting another, although the knowable remains forever elusive. This is lyrically expressed by Martin Buber as

> both moments are unfolded fatefully in time and enclosed, as by grace, in the timeless creation that, incomprehensively, is at once release and preservation, at once bond and liberation. Our knowledge of duality is reduced to silence by the paradox of the primal mystery.
>
> — Martin Buber, *I and Thou*, tr. Walter Kaufmann

While paying heed to this mystery Dr Sharma reformulates

the concept of empathy by drawing on the presence of Kantian notions of a priori structure such that empathy is likened to an independent mental act which is episodic as it relates to and draws on other mental processes such as introspection as well as related psychological constructs such as countertransference. In developing a unique psychological notion of empathy, Dr Sharma draws on the notion of positive projective identification wherein a representation of oneself is juxtaposed against that of another, i.e. double representation in linguistic and non-linguistic forms. The fluidity of this process is elaborated on by drawing on the analogy of a potential space wherein transitional concepts are drawn from, thereby highlighting the complexity of the perceptual process.

I am happy to be associated with this project and it is my firm belief that the study will generate much interest and discussion, as it has already begun to in the Australasian context.

Sidney Bloch
Professor (Clinical) and
Professor, Department of Psychiatry
The University of Melbourne, St Vincent's Hospital, and
Former Editor, *Journal of the Royal Australian and New Zealand College of Psychiatry*

Contents

Introduction

THE significance of understanding empathy cannot be overemphasized. In this study Dr Renuka Sharma shows how empathy can provide insight into another person's mental states, not accessible otherwise. Viewed from this perspective, empathy can be used as a clinical tool in a therapeutic setting. Sharma well shows the way in which using empathy as a means of diagnosis led her to a different, more successful course of action. Thus, there is an epistemological and an ethical component in practising empathy. The interest in empathy spans across disciplines, and studying empathy promises a deeper understanding of human communication, relations and action.

Sharma first provides a thorough historical and etymological account of the origin and uses of the term "empathy" in various disciplines. She then proceeds to discuss the literature on empathy in psychoanalysis. There is no shortage of literature defining empathy which Sharma carefully surveys to provide the reader with an up to date map of the issues in professional literature. Sharma fully explains the extent and limitations of the material available. She notes that the research is insufficient and consequently the definition of empathy available is unsatisfactory. The emphasis in psychoanalysis is on the affective aspect of empathy, and yet because empathy is a tool to inquire into the life of another, a satisfactory account of empathy must be predominately an epistemological one. Even though empathy does seems to play a role in various therapeutic stances, it is not sufficiently differentiated from other psychoanalytic terms such as identification, countertransference, projection, introjection and projective identification. Last, there are also challenges in studying empathy as the concept can be ellusive scientifically.

Sharma is in a unique position to approach the topic. Familiar with both the literatures in psychoanalysis and philosophy, she takes an interdisciplinary approach, combining a conceptual analysis mainly drawing from phenomenology with empirical data collected in a clinical setting. The clarity with which she is able to formulate the mechanism of empathy and her access to clinical cases lend itself to a more solid theory that can be articulated and further studied.

First we turn to the foundation of this study, the conceptual framework for understanding empathy where the author's originality and significant contribution to this field lie. The question is clearly raised: given that there are boundaries between self and other, between subject and object, how does empathy provide an epistemic understanding of the reality of the other? Sharma is successful in answering this question in locating empathy in intersubjectivity, to which we turn next.

Conceptual Analysis of Empathy

The author notes that thus far in the literature on psychoanalysis psychic reality is located within *intrasubjective space* (within the individual). She challenges this view with her concept of intersubjectivity where she locates empathy. The term *intersubjective space* is used to denote a psychic reality occurring between two people. It is an experience that is neither subjective, nor objective, and, more simply put, denotes an experience of a relation between two people. Empathy, she explains, is an intersubjective phenomenon. As such, empathy necessarily takes into account both the reality of the self and that of another. Appraising another through empathy includes an appraisal of self in relation to another. Thus knowing the other or understanding the reality of another is gained in two ways — introspection and perception. Empathy is constituted through the interplay of introspection and perception. Sharma labels this a process of "double representation". She distinguishes between and among the cognitive, affective and perceptive aspects of empathy. In Sharma's own words the cognitive aspect pans out as follows:

> My proposal is that the cognitive aspect involved in this process occurs by means of "double representation". Thus, a representation of self, be that in the form of memory, experience, part object, imagination, or linguistic trace, is juxtaposed with a collateral representation of the other. On the basis of congruence, deductions are made about similarities to oneself and, on the basis on non-congruence, an openness allows for difference. – p. 78

In other words, the representation of the self alongside the other leads to information concerning both the similarities and differences between the observer and the observed. Information regarding another person gained through empathy appears in the form of a mental representation and Sharma proceeds to demonstrate the process with empirical data obtained in a clinical setting. She sites a case in which a young Asian male was admitted to the hospital after a suicide attempt following a separation from his girlfriend. During the intake, the young man giggled, a reaction that would normally seem inappropriate. But empathy reveals otherwise. Through introspection Sharma was able to access her own memory and understanding of the meaning of psychiatry in Asian culture and was able to explain the giggle as "metonymic device of deferral". Through perception she was able to understand the patient on his own terms, given that there are differences such as gender, culture and education, all of which are important components of being able to understand the reasons behind the suicide attempt.

Sharma continues to explain the affective and perceptual aspects of empathy, their epistemological value and practical application as clinical tools. In clinical terms the affective aspect of empathy is transmitted in a way akin to "mature projective identification". In lay persons' terms she describes the process as a "gut feeling". Sharma cites a case of a woman who suffered from catatonic schizophrenia and was unresponsive. Sharma could feel her forlornness and despair. In response, She informed the patient that they would speak only when it is comfortable and safe enough to do so. It took three days and the patient did begin to talk; it seems that the patient was able to communicate some of her affects in this way. It was a "gut feeling" that led Sharma to this form of treatment as opposed to leaving the patient alone until she was ready to speak. The perceptive aspect of empathy is neither cognitive nor affective, but consists in observing behaviour in order to gain insight into a patient's imagination and fantasies. Here Sharma cites a very interesting case, in which she observed a schizophrenic patient, who has been institutionalized for most of his life, stare into the staff room for hours. Curious about this odd behaviour, Sharma began inquiring about his dreams and fantasies and it turns out that this patient dreamed of being a writer and attempted to do so on various occasions. As a result the patient was gradually provided with a typewriter, a desk and a briefcase. He was able to write to different organizations, Amnesty International and others, and even received a volunteer to take him out shopping.

In all her case studies Sharma shows how empathy, whether cognitive, affective or perceptive, helped her diagnose and respond to patients in a way that pure logic would fall short. Empathy turned out to be invaluable in cases of unresponsive or severely disturbed patients where a conversation could not take place. This work bears striking common denominators with feminist philosophy. In what follows Sharma's affinity to feminist epistemology and feminist ethics will be pursued.

Renuka Sharma and Feminist Epistemology

Feminist epistemology is a vast field containing many themes, some are even not unique to feminist literature. The comparison here is confined to two pertinent points. One, emotions provide an added way of knowing, and two, by their nature emotions provide contextual knowledge. Alison Jaggar in "Love and Knowledge: Emotions in Feminist Epistemology" notes that reason as a way of knowing has been dominant in Western epistemology especially from the seventeenth century onward, whereas emotions have been discounted as a source of knowledge.[1] In order to show the epistemological component of emotions Jaggar presents emotions in a different light. Emotions are intentional (we are angry about something). Emotions both presuppose a value and suggest one. It is certainly appropriate to feel anger and indignation in the face of human rights violations; it is also another way of perceiving the wrongness of the situation. Emotions are also socially constructed; we are taught what to fear and what to value. Emotions then partake in our evaluations and observations. Jaggar argues that understanding the information gained through emotions is helpful and even necessary in the construction of knowledge. She reminds us that Jane's Goodall's scientific understating of chimpanzees was made possible through her added empathy and even love for these animals.

Similarly Margaret Walker in "Moral Understanding: Alternative 'Epistemology' for Feminist Ethics" writes that the history of ethics has been dominated by the search for moral knowledge such as universal moral rules.[2] General and abstract

---

[1] *Inquiry*, **32**(2): 151-76 (1989).

[2] *Hypatia*, **4**(2): 15-25 (1989).

rules do not always help with real people in specific situations. Instead, Walker offers her concept of moral understanding as a foundation for feminist ethics. Moral understanding consists of attention to particular persons, and as such it is a contextual and narrative understanding of people instead of a general and abstract one. Thus, rather than discerning general moral rules, one looks specifically at people's beliefs, feelings and modes of expression to construct a story which would enable us to respond to their particular needs.

Both points are seen in Sharma's work. The first, the epistemological value of emotions is found in her actual augment; and the second, the contextual and narrative understanding is seen in her practice. In the case studies sighted, empathy provided an understanding of the patients not gained by reason, in line with claims in feminist literature that emotions provide an additional way of knowing. Empathy also enabled Sharma to consider her patients on a case by case basis and take a different therapeutic course of action. Acting on the dictates of empathy points to an ethical dimension in Sharma's work which deserves separate attention.

Sharma and Feminist Ethics

It is an interesting coincidence that I was asked to write this introduction when Sharma bears similarities to an eighteenth-century woman philosopher, Sophie de Grouchy's, concept of sympathy, with which I am very familiar. De Grouchy (1764–1822) translated Adam Smith's *The Theory of Moral Sentiments* into French and she appended eight *Letters on Sympathy* to her translation. Her translation of Smith remained the standard translation in French for two centuries; the last edition was published in 1982 (although without the *Letters*).

Sharma acknowledges that what Hume had to say about sympathy, namely that people can communicate their sentiments through sympathy, applies to empathy as well. The same claim can be made about de Grouchy's concept of sympathy. De Grouchy provides the following explanation for the origin of sympathy. Experiences of physical or emotional pain leave a lasting impression beyond the specific occurrences, which de Grouchy labels "a general impression of pain". This general impression can be recalled by the sight or memory of pain, and we can experience a painful memory.

> In the same way as the memory of an injury we have felt reproduces the painful impression . . . so, too, we feel this painful impression again when, being in a position to notice the signs of pain.[3]

Following this explanation, de Grouchy defines sympathy "as disposition we have to feel as others do". Similar to Sharma's formulation of double representation, for de Grouchy understanding the suffering of others requires a perception of their pain combined with a memory of our own. The component of memory in de Grouchy and introspection in Sharma elucidates the way in which sympathy/empathy leads to an understanding of another through the self. We perceive another and through tapping into our own experience a component of feeling emerges, essentially we are identifying with another.

Nona Lyons, in her article "Two Perspectives: On Self, Relationships and Morality" notes that in the studies she conducted males and females manifested two different modes of perceiving themselves in relation to others, which lead to different concepts of morality. Males tend to view themselves as separate and independent of others, and thus think of morality in terms of reciprocity, which results in a perspective

---

[3] Sophie de Grouchy, *Letters on Sympathy (1798): A Critical Edition*, Karin Brown and James E. McClellan III, American Philosophical Society, 2008, p. 109.

of justice; whereas females tend to view themselves as connected to others; thus they think in terms of response, which results in an ethics of care. The perspective of response Lyons writes "is based on interdependence and concern for another's well-being".[4] An ethics of response leads to attending to the needs of others. The distinction between the separate view of individuals and the connectedness and relational views of persons resembles Sharma's distinction between intrasubjectivity and intersubjectivity. The relational views of persons in terms of response is seen in Sharma's course of action in therapy. Although Sharma did not explicitly elaborate on the ethical implications of her theory, they are clearly seen in the result of using empathy in therapy. In her case studies empathy led her to think outside the box which resulted in remarkable achievements with her patients.

Further

Ranuka successfully undertakes the challenge of elucidating the complex phenomenon of empathy. Combining the cognitive, affective and perceptual aspects of empathy, the reader comes to understand empathy as a reciprocal process between knowing and feeling. Upon perceiving another and considering our own experiences, similarities and differences are understood; affect emerges and further informs the deductions made by reason. What was seen in a clinical setting, namely the way in which empathy functioned as a way of knowing and as a moral emotion, is applicable beyond therapeutic use to human relations at large. For further study, Sharma suggests a possible link between intersubjectivity and the Buddhist notion of compassion. Such an investigation is a subject for an entirely new project, which unfortunately due to Sharma's untimely passing did not come to fruition. One can say that Sharma possessed the insight that compassion

[4] *Harvard Educational Review*, **53**(2): 125-45 (1983).

requires a specific epistemological foundation of understanding the other, which one can find in Buddhist philosophy. More recently, Allan B. Wallace in his article "Intersubjectivity in Indo-Tibetan Buddhism" explains that the concept of the self in Buddhist philosophy arises in interdependence as a result of causes and conditions.[5] As such, Wallace claims that the very concept of the self is intersubjective. Moreover, Wallace writes that the concept of the self is constructed through empathy. Wallace uses the term "reiterated empathy" to denote a process through which we learn about ourselves through a second person's perspective. Compassion is based on empathy since it is a result of being empathically attentive to another. The connection between intersubjectivity and empathy is already well established in Sharma's work, the foundation for compassion, although not stated, does clearly follow.

In this work, Sharma provides a clear account of the mechanism of empathy and shows the application in a clinical setting. In doing so, she lays the foundation for further discussion. It is indeed my hope that this work serves as a prolegomenon to future research in empathy.

San Jose State University
California (USA)

Karin Brown, Ph.D
Associate Professor of philosophy

---

[5] *Journal of Consciousness Studies*, **8:** 1-22 (2001).

1

Empathy:
A Historical Perspective

HISTORICALLY the term "empathy" entered the English language from its occurrence in German aesthetics. Following this specific usage and adaptation, the meaning of the term has become broadened to include many areas of concern and study, most of which fall outside the scope of the present inquiry. The term is not only used in a number of symbolic ways but it also touches on epistemological issues within certain disciplines.

But the history is even longer: its origins take us back to Greek poetics. The word *empatheia* appears in Aristotle's *Rhetoric*, nuanced here in an animistic sense. It was subsequently used to describe the specific quality that affords one an appreciation of art. On the question of the use of the term closer to the present era, a number of different historical accounts is given in the literature.[1] It appears, however, that the term empathy is connected with the German word *Einfühlung*, literally "infeeling" used in the late nineteenth century to describe a form of aesthetic perception.

---

[1] J.B. Hunsdahl, "Concerning Einfühlung (Empathy): A Conceptual Analysis of Its Origins and Early Development", *Journal of the History of the Behavioral Sciences*, **3**: 180-91, 1967; G.H. Northrup, *Psychoanalytic Issues in the Theory of Empathy* (Dissertation), Michigan: University Microfilms International, 1986 (Microfiche).

Etymologically, the term was derived from *empatheia* to translate the German word *Einfühlung*. It was used in this context by Friedrich Theodor Vischer and subsequently by Violet Paget and Theodor Lipps. Lipps, however, was not the first to use the term as is often thought. A book by F.R. Vischer which appeared in 1873 attests to the earliest printed occurrence of the term. Reference is also made to the work of Friedrich Theodor Vischer (father of F.R. Vischer), prior to the first published reference, in the field of aesthetics around 1846.[2] It is important to note that although the term originated around 1846, the concept itself could probably be traced back to earlier times, such as in the ideas of Vico and Hume on beauty and sympathy.[3] Hume spoke of sympathy as "a propensity . . . to receive by communication (others') inclinations and sentiments, however different from, or even contrary, to our own".[4] Hume's interest in sympathy was focused mainly on its implications for ethical judgement and for the moral motivation in caring about the suffering or sorrow of another. While Hume did not intend to subsume empathy under sympathy, what he had to say about sympathy extends in larger measure to empathy as well, with the difference that sympathy all too often leads to a display of the emotion and possibly also action as a considered (moral) response to the other's situation.[5] The important differences will be adverted to rather than spelt out in this work.

---

[2] J.B. Hunsdahl, "Concerning Einfühlung (Empathy): A Conceptual Analysis of Its Origins and Early Development", *Journal of the History of the Behavioral Sciences*, **3**: 180-91, 1967.

[3] I. Berlin, *Vico and Herder: Two Studies in the History of Ideas*, New York: Viking, 1976.

[4] David Hume, *Enquiries Concerning Human Understanding and Concerning the Principles of Morals (1978)*, rev. edn., Oxford: Clarendon Press, 1975, p. 189; David Hume, *A Treatise of Human Nature* (1741; 2.1.9-11), rev. edn., Oxford: Clarendon Press, 1978.

[5] P. Bilimoria, "Ethics of Emotions: Some Crosscultural →

Theodor Lipps' original use of the German term *Einfühlung* in his work *Aesthetic*, published in 1903, related to the appreciation of inanimate works of art.[6] This initial use was later expanded to include the understanding of other individuals, and curiously it coincides with the present definition of the word "projection". Lipps defined *Einfühlung* as a process of projection and identification with an object of art. This internalized representation of the object led to closer understanding of the object, which was thought to occur by means of motor mimicry.

As well as writing on empathy, Lipps was also concerned with understanding the dynamic conception of the unconscious as psychic energy. Moritz Geiger, a student of Lipps, wrote his dissertation on the problem of the unconscious on phenomenological grounds.[7] Lipps also had an influence on Karl Jaspers. This early groundswell of ideas led to the subsequent development in different directions. Margulies,[8] comparing Husserl's notion of phenomenological reduction to Freud's concept of free-floating attention, notices certain similarities in the attempt by both to get to the "essence" of consciousness, in both its conscious and unconscious modes of experiencing or being-in-the-world.

→ Reflections", in J. Marks and R. Ames (eds.) *Emotions: East & West*, NY: SUNY Press, Spring 1994.

6 Theodor Lipps, *Aesthetik*, Hamburg: Voss, 1903; Theodor Lipps, "Empathy and Aesthetic Pleasure" (tr. Karl Aschenbrenner, 1903), in *Aesthetic Theories: Studies in the Philosophy of Art*, ed. Karl Aschenbrenner and Arnold Isenberg, Englewood Cliff, NJ: Prentice Hall, 1965, pp. 403-12.

7 Herbert Spiegelberg, *Phenomenology in Psychology and Psychiatry: A Historical Introduction*, Evanston: Northwestern University Press, 1972.

8 A. Margulies and L.L. Havens, "The Initial Encounter: What to Do First?", *American Journal of Psychiatry*, **138**(4): 421-28, 1981.

By 1910, Edward B. Titchener had rendered the literal meaning of the phrase "feeling oneself into" with the English word empathy.[9] Violet Paget had earlier translated *Einfühlung* as "sympathy", intending to mean "feeling for", not empathy, and she herself attributes the translation to Titchener.[10] (The etymological root *sym* is to do with "together" and *pathos* with "suffering, feeling, pain".) But it was the introduction of the term by Lipps in the last century that led to its varying uses in a number of different disciplines.[11] Hence, while Lipps was not the first, nor the last, to develop a theory of empathy, he was nevertheless responsible for developing it extensively as a psychological concept, and it was with this development that its future impact was mapped out. Lipps, then, can be seen as being an early influential figure on later developments in phenomenology and psychology. It is ironic, though, that the subsequent study of empathy, as we shall see, has been subsumed by the study of intersubjectivity in philosophy and the domain of empirical psychology and psychoanalysis, instead of its continued location within the field of phenomenological psychology.

Of interest also is the use of the term in a number of rather disparate fields of inquiry. Apart from providing an ongoing

[9] G.H. Northrup, *Psychoanalytic Issues in the Theory of Empathy* (Dissertation), Michigan: University Microfilms International, 1986 (Microfiche).

[10] J.B. Hunsdahl, "Concerning Einfühlung (Empathy): A Conceptual Analysis of Its Origins and Early Development", *Journal of the History of the Behavioral Sciences*, **3**: 180-91, 1967; G.H. Northrup, *Psychoanalytic Issues in the Theory of Empathy* (Dissertation), Michigan: University Microfilms International, 1986 (Microfiche).

[11] Theodor Lipps, *Aesthetik*, Hamburg: Voss, 1903; Theodor Lipps, "Empathy and Aesthetic Pleasure" (tr. Karl Aschenbrenner, 1903), in *Aesthetic Theories: Studies in the Philosophy of Art*, ed. Karl Aschenbrenner and Arnold Isenberg, Englewood Cliff, NJ: Prentice Hall, 1965, pp. 403-12.

conceptual structure within the field of aesthetics, in cross-cultural studies, such as in sociology/anthropology and religion, the term "empathy" has been used as a tool to gain access to subject areas of inquiry that may be at some psychological or cultural distance and variance with the observer's point of reference. The works of Max Weber, Evans-Pritchard, Bronisław Milanowski and Martin Buber come to mind here, as does Gerardus van der Leeuw's so-called phenomenology of religion, wherein he popularized the methodological equivalent of the German *Verstehen* as a means of gaining an understanding of the "insider's" or the believer's world-view while bracketing all judgements and moral evaluations. Philosophers nowadays are generally of the view that most if not all of the emotions directly or indirectly involve a "moral point of view" or ethical judgement in respect of the situation, person or event to which the felt emotion is a response. The case is clearer in the instance of guilt and anger — moral indignation — but perhaps less so in the emotions such as compassion, love and aesthetic *jouissance* (cf. Solomon[12]).

More recently, the term empathy has also been used in relation to the study of literary deconstruction, by people such as Blanchard, in order to arrive at the meaning of written texts.[13]

Within the domain of philosophy, empathy was commented on in relation to intersubjectivity. Herbert Spiegelberg, in a comprehensive historical account of the cross-currents between psychology and phenomenology, identifies

---

[12] Robert C. Solomon, *The Passions*, NY: Doubleday/Anchor, 1977.

[13] W. Tatarkiewicz and M. Golebiowski, "Aesthetic Experience: The Early History of the Concept" *Dialectics and Humanism*, Autumn 1973, pp. 19-30; J.D. Bettis (ed.), *Phenomenology of Religion: Eight Modem Descriptions of the Essence of Religion*, New York: Harper & Row, 1969; Martin Buber, *Between Man and Man*, New York: Macmillan, 1965; J. H.Kultgen, "Defence of Verstehen", *Personalist*, **53**: 170-87, 1972; S.N. Lawall, *Critics of Consciousness: The Existential Structures of Literature*, Cambridge, MA: Harvard University Press, 1968.

empathy as one of the early issues addressed by both disciplines.[14] Thus, empathy was commented on extensively by the phenomenologists and psychologists of the early 1900s. However, only in the past thirty years has it been reconsidered within psychoanalysis, as well as by the proponents of Self-Psychology, who are now reappraising the early philosophical basis of empathy.[15] Thus, it is relevant to note that interest in empathy has arisen with an interest in Self-Psychology, leading to a re-examination of the philosophical roots of empathy.[16] To recapitulate, briefly, I shall examine the early philosophical origins of the concept within phenomenology.

Phenomenology grew out of Franz Brentano's attempt to develop a conception of experience as something more than sensation-bound or a collection of sense-data impressions. He focused his inquiry on a deeper analysis of the structure of perception as one instance of a wide variety of experiences. Brentano distinguished this particular form of perception from introspection and deliberate self-examination on the basis of the function of representation by consciousness in all its modalities. Thus, this early form of phenomenology was based on the description of representations within consciousness, while acknowledging the complexity of the structure more than had been admitted, for example, in the empiricists' or Locke's representational theory of perception.[17]

---

[14] Herbert Spiegelberg, *Phenomenology in Psychology and Psychiatry: A Historical Introduction*, Evanston: Northwestern University Press, 1972.

[15] R.D. Stolorow and G.E. Atwood, "The Work of Stolorow and Atwood" Symposium Psychoanalytic Phenomenology (reply to R. White, M. Basch and M. Nissam Sabat), **73**(3): 301-08, 1986.

[16] Renuka M. Sharma, "Empathy: A Retrospective on Its Development in Psychotherapy", *Australian and New Zealand Journal of Psychiatry*, **26**(3): 377-90, 1993.

[17] Ron Harré (ed.), *The Encyclopaedia Dictionary of Psychology*, Oxford: Basil Blackwell, 1983.

Edmund Husserl and Sigmund Freud were both students of Brentano at approximately the same period of time. Although Freud does not acknowledge either, he acknowledges the work of Theodor Lipps, the contemporary phenomenologist whose work was attacked by Husserl as a chief exponent of psychologism. In spite of this, Husserl was later to take Lipps' concept of empathy and modify it. Edith Stein, a student and collaborator of Husserl, extended the work on empathy. The related concept of sympathy was taken up by Max Scheler whose main interest at that time centred on the phenomenology of the emotions.[18]

Following on from the early discussion within psychology, in the beginning of the nineteenth century, there were frequent references to the term empathy in the psychoanalytic literature and this led to a resurgence of interest in the middle decades of this century. Several essays and papers on the subject were brought together in two volumes published in the 1980s.[19] A third collated work, generated within the domain of cognitive psychology, also appeared by Goldtsein and Michaels.[20] Both approaches detailed the difficulties in defining the term and the possible misuses within the various research attempts, while exploring developmental studies and the implications of a more comprehensive understanding for therapy.

In the following year, Northrup completed his work outlining the polemical positions taken up in relation to the

---

[18] Herbert Spiegelberg, *Phenomenology in Psychology and Psychiatry: A Historical Introduction*, Evanston: Northwestern University Press, 1972; Edith Stein, *On the Problem of Empathy*, tr. W. Stein, The Hague: Martinus Nijhoff, 1964; Max Scheler, *The Nature of Sympathy*, tr. Peter Heath, Hamden, CI: Archon Books, 1954.

[19] J. Lichtenberg, M. Bornstein, and D. Silver (eds.), *Empathy I and II* (2 vols), Hillsdale, NJ: The Analytic Press, 1984.

[20] A.P. Goldstein and Y.G Michaels, *Empathy, Development, Training and Consequences*, Hillsdale, NJ: Lawrence Erlbaum, 1985.

term within the boundaries of psychoanalysis.[21] His contribution appears as a signpost within the historical perspective of this concept in that a detailed examination of the polemics reveals further conflict with both the language and politics of psychoanalysis, and also points to fundamental epistemological problems concerned with ways of knowing within psychoanalysis.

To recapitulate: from the early, albeit brief, expression in Greek classic literature, the term "empathy" has come to be used in a number of varying contexts. Later it was a term that was frequently used within the field of aesthetics, and at the turn of this century the concept of empathy attracted the attention of researchers in the (overlapping) areas of phenomenology and psychoanalysis. The term continues to be used today in these disciplines along with other varied usages in comparative religions, cross-cultural studies, anthropology, psychology and literary deconstruction. The early, albeit obtuse, definitions and their continued use in a number of different ways shed light on the variety of ways in which empathy it has been construed within psychoanalysis.

It may be important then not to look for a single, all-encompassing definition of empathy, but rather to contend with multiple meanings and a plurality of frames, varying according to the contexts and the intentionality of those who use the term or embed the concept in the structure of feeling and understanding. The analogy of an hermeneutic circle may help to make more comprehensible the shades of meaning that this term seems to have acquired in psychoanalytic literature. With the rise of Self-Psychology in the past thirty years, there has been an increasing discussion of the concept

---

[21] G.H. Northrup, *Psychoanalytic Issues in the Theory of Empathy* (Dissertation), Michigan: University Microfilms International, 1986 (Microfiche).

and its relationship to inquiries in related fields. The emphasis on interpersonal connotations came much later, and it is in this light that the concept of empathy has received considerable interest since the 1950s. There have, of course, been alternative viewpoints from outside the psychoanalytic field, notably in behavioural, cognitive and biological sciences. For instance, Leslie Brothers[22] formulates a significant biological perspective on empathy. Some of these contributions will be discussed in the subsequent chapters.

---

[22] L. Brothers, "A Biological Perspective on Empathy", *American Journal of Psychiatry*, **146**(1): 10-17, 1989.

2

Problems with Psychoanalytic Definitions of Empathy

Having retraced the origins of the term "empathy" via its historico-archaeological episteme, I wish now to turn to the large body of psychoanalytic writing on the subject of empathy, which shows certain internal inconsistencies in its attempt to grapple with the notion which was appropriated from a rather different praxis. Despite the amount of attention given to the concept in the past thirty years, the theoretical status appears as ambiguous as ever. This is the central finding and conclusion arrived at in this study.

In 1986 George H. Northrup,[1] hitherto an unknown researcher in the field, produced a landmark study in the form of a dissertation raising several issues on psychoanalytic understanding of empathy. His detailed examination of the concept reveals tensions both in the language and politics of psychoanalysis, and points to certain fundamental epistemological problems within psychoanalysis. Northrup suggests in this study that, in spite of seventy-nine years of clinical reflection, empathy "remains an estranged concept in psychoanalysis".[2] Some of the issues are addressed in important ways in Shapiro's contributions to the discussion as well.

---

1 G.H. Northrup, *Psychoanalytic Issues in the Theory of Empathy* (Dissertation), Michigan: University Microfilms International, 1986 (Microfiche).

2 Ibid.

Numerous formulations have been put forth to explain the concept. The ambivalence may have to do, in part, with the characterization of empathy as inherently a non-rational, emotionally charged (bordering on the *effemint*) and non-scientific phenomenon, *vis-à-vis* its rationalization within psychoanalytic thinking as a scientific or quasi-scientific technique. I shall briefly remark on the tensions and polemics in more recent efforts to deal with the problematic before moving on, in the chapters to follow, to illustrate my thesis with a more detailed historical analysis of its treatment in psychoanalytic discourse from Freud onwards.

Unconscious Polemics

Gail Reed,[3] writing on "The Antithetical Meaning of the Term 'Empathy' in Psychoanalytic Discourse", points out that when the different definitions of the word are juxtaposed a number of dichotomous positions emerge. Reed's paper offers a psychoanalytic understanding of the various schismatic viewpoints and a psychoanalytic interpretation in terms indicating either oedipal or dyadic conflict unconsciously present in discussions on empathy. In the event of these conflicts remaining unacknowledged by individuals and more collectively by the profession, the risk of "closure to meaningful dialogue around a critical psychoanalytic concept" remains (Schwaber 1984).[4]

These diametric positions, according to Reed, fall roughly into the two following groups: the active, scientific and

---

[3] Gail S. Reed, "The Antithetical Meaning of the Term 'Empathy' in Psychoanalytic Discourse", in *Empathy I* (ed. Lichtenberg J. et al.), Hillsdale, NJ: The Analytic Press, 1984, pp. 7-24.

[4] E. Schwaber, "Discussion", in *Empathy I* (ed. Lichtenberg J. et al.), pp. 25-30.

thrusting metaphors relating to a capacity for fathering versus the passive, mystical and encompassing metaphors relating to mothering. She suggests that these may represent underlying fantasies shared by the users of the term in either collective, academic or ordinary usage. It is interesting to reflect that these positions may indicate gender differences, or, more generally, inclinations in the capacity to empathize.

Evelyn Schwaber, while agreeing with Reed, points out the dangers of positioning the therapist as observer outside the field of observation and thus creating artificial distinctions that are introduced by the perspective of the viewer (the "insider", the "native"). Thus, Schwaber seems to suggest that the unconscious premises of the observer influence the perception of the "other" person being empathized with.

Schafer,[5] responding to Reed, states that the options of definition are either to set up antithetic polarities or to construct multidimensional encompassing models. Neither model, "disjunctive" or "conjunctive", allows for a blend of the opposites. Furthermore, the inconsistency in discussing empathy is a characteristic of the discussion of other major analytic terms, such as identification, which is described both as process and the end result of the process. This raises a number of issues relating to the study of objective realities, or, in the context of empathy, the study of another's reality. The problem of a subject–object difference as commented on by Schwaber is again raised with the additional problem of how subjective realities could be best studied.

It may be surmised that the problem of definition is far greater with a term such as empathy, since the processes and structures are not only close to unconscious modes of thought, but a description by an observer or analyst in a therapeutic

---

[5] Roy Schafer, "Discussion", in *Empathy I* (ed. Lichtenberg J. et al.), pp. 31-36.

setting also involves references to that analyst's private language, and hence includes the intersubjective contribution to the description. As such, definitions are idiosyncratic and suggest the therapist's own fantasies and tensions as well as a perception of the subject–other, requiring a delicate balance of perspectives in working with a particular patient. Schafer maintains that a continued attempt at definition will need an understanding of the distinctions between introspective and objective knowledge, leading to a better description and understanding of the mechanisms, origins and psychic placement of this component of the "work ego". This distinction between objective and subjective components of empathy is developed by Northrup.[6]

Spence[7] sees the confusion arising as a result of the use of the term to cover a number of other psychoanalytic terms, such as free association, evenly hovering attention, atmosphere and interpretation. However, it seems that a clearer differentiation of the term can only occur if the unconscious factors in defining the term are acknowledged.

Epistemological Polemics

To inquire into the life of another is, in the deepest sense, an inquiry into the reality of the other, so it is in this sense that a theory of empathy is, or must be, an epistemological theory. Such an inquiry will not reveal the entire reality of the other but only a part. An understanding of the reality of the other is gained in two main ways, neither of which operates in isolation from the other, i.e. introspection and perception.

---

6 G.H. Northrup, *Psychoanalytic Issues in the Theory of Empathy* (Dissertation), Michigan: University Microfilms International, 1986 (Microfiche).

7 J.H. Spence Jr, "Discussion", in *Empathy I* (ed. Lichtenberg J. et al.), pp. 37-42.

Introspection and perception, as I interpret these here, are not to be confused with free association and evenly hovering attention, respectively. To explore the definitions of subjective and objective reality as well as the form and processes is pertinent to the present discussion, but this task is beyond the confines of the present work.

The epistemological status of empathy has been commented on by a number of writers. Freud made brief reference to the problem of subject–object distinction in relation to empathy, Kohut commented on this aspect of empathy extensively, and more recently Northrup, Margulies, Meares and Agosta have explored aspects of the epistemological status of empathy.[8]

Traditionally, the boundaries between subject and object were thought to be definable by mechanical rules and studied under the laws of causality. However, with an awareness of the laws of relativity, the historical and cultural embeddedness of all knowledge is being increasingly acknowledged. Thus,

---

[8] Sigmund Freud, "Group Psychology and the Analysis of the Ego", in *Complete Psychology Works of Sigmund Freud,* ed. and tr. J. Strachey (standard edn.), London: Hogarth Press, 1955, vol. 18, pp. 69-144; Heinz Kohut, "Introspection, Empathy, and Psychoanlysis: An Examination of the Relationship Between Mode of Observation and Theory", *Journal of American Psychoanal. Association*, **7**: 459-83, 1959; Heinz Kohut, "Introspection, Empathy and the Semicircle of Mental Health", *International Journal of Psycho-Analysis*, **63**: 395-408, 1982; G.H. Northrup, *Psychoanalytic Issues in the Theory of Empathy* (Dissertation), Michigan: University Microfilms International, 1986 (Microfiche); A. Margulies, "Towards Empathy: The Uses of Wonder", *American Journal of Psychiatry*, **141**(9): 1025-33, 1984; Russell Meares, "Keats and the 'Impersonal' Therapist: A Note on Empathy and the Therapeutic Screen", *Psychiatry*, **46**: 73-82, February 1983; L. Agosta, "Empathy and Intersubjectivity", in *Empathy I* (ed. Lichtenberg J. et al.), pp. 43-62.

it is recognized that a study of empathy should at least include an examination of its initial occurrence and history, and its uses and abuses within a therapeutic setting. The location of psychic reality within intrasubjective spaces in isolation from other influences is challenged by this emerging perspective. Thus, an empathic appraisal of another necessarily includes an appraisal of self in relation to other.

The location of empathy in the intersubjective space allows for an acknowledgement of this relativity and has implications for a greater understanding of the transference as well as the real therapeutic relationship. As an intersubjective phenomenon it takes into account the reality of the other as well as of the self. As such it is a unique phenomenon that allows for a cognizance of self and other simultaneously. Defined as a category of experience that is neither subjective nor objective but is an experience of another in relation to the self, it has affinity to the psychoanalytic notion of counter-transference, which will be discussed later.

Empathy can thus be framed as being composed of both forms of observations, so that "no empathy without an external agent and no object without extrospection" is possible.[9] This dynamic interplay between perception and introspection is often forgotten and appears to account for some of the semantic and epistemological confusions in various definitions of empathy. Kohut was aware of this complexity. In his paper on "Introspection, empathy and mental health"[10] he states that "empathy and introspection are often linked and amalgamated with other modes of observation". From this perspective,

---

[9] G.H. Northrup, *Psychoanalytic Issues in the Theory of Empathy* (Dissertation), Michigan: University Microfilms International, 1986 (Microfiche).

[10] Heinz Kohut, "Introspection, Empathy and the Semicircle of Mental Health", *International Journal of Psycho-Analysis*, **63**: 395-408, 1982.

empathy can be defined as a synthesis of both forms of knowing (the other), such that pure sense-data are integrated with affective and cognitive, conscious and unconscious introspective data, resulting in inferences about the inner world of the other. Stated another way, this integration involves primary (fantasy) and secondary (logical) process thinking. The analogy of Bion's grid of thinking can be used to explicate the mechanisms of integration of primary processes with higher-order thinking, leading to concept formation.[11]

In the therapeutic setting, the integration of external reality "with inner streams of consciousness" results in a greater depth of understanding of another. These inferences, initially, are limited to the understanding of the immediate reality of another, which over time give way to an understanding of genetic, developmental influences and transferential aspects of the relationship, leading eventually to formulations about the other's personality.

If a single implication were to be distilled from the foregoing assessment, it would be that the process of empathy can provide a better understanding of the intersubjective aspects of the immediate as well as the intersubjective aspects of transference relationship within a therapeutic situation. Thus it follows that different instances and interactions call for different levels of psychological understandings that could be implemented by the empathic technique. Whereas an analysis of transference may be appropriate in a given setting, some would argue that empathic understanding without interpretation may be useful in the case of more severely disturbed patients. This view follows from Kohut's studies on the clinical application of empathy that combines observation and introspection.

---

[11] W.R. Bion, *Learning from Experience*, London: Maresfield Reprints, 1962.

It also follows that a plurality of ways of understanding another, without the danger of relativism or nihilism, may be made possible if the complexity of the processes involved in an empathic appraisal is duly countenanced. Simple reliance on sense-data input may prove to be meaningless and, on introspection, entirely solipsistic. Thus empathy appears to be an intersubjective event which is noetic, in that as a mode of perception external reality is also taken into account. Seen in these terms, empathy becomes a useful clinical and epistemological tool that attempts to locate the imaged "other" in the matrix of the intersubjective relation between self and other. Also, in this regard, claims for a pure scientific study of empathy lose meaning, as do attempts to label empathy as entirely mystical, non-scientific or irrational. Instead, a theory is required that has internal consistency and parsimony as well as allowing for an understanding of clinical phenomenon.

Semantic Polemics

It is postulated that the ambiguity in defining empathy may have been perpetuated by a failure to define the term in relation to existing psychoanalytic terms, such as countertransference, regression, projective identification and introjection, and that it remains largely disembodied from the paradigm of psychoanalytic thought.[12] However, as discussed above, inherent difficulties in defining the component parts of the process of empathy may be reflected in the multitude of definitions and semantic perspectives that have become stock-in-trade. These perspectives raise a number of complex and relevant issues that have been briefly addressed in the previous chapter. Of more relevance to a clinical definition other issues

---

[12] J.H. Spence Jr, "Discussion", in *Empathy I* (ed. Lichtenberg J. et al.), pp. 37-42; G.H. Northrup, *Psychoanalytic Issues in the Theory of Empathy* (Dissertation), Michigan: University Microfilms International, 1986 (Microfiche).

emerge, basically concerning the nature of the description, as follows: Is empathy about experience near or experience distant phenomena? Is it about distinctions between conscious and unconscious affect and fantasy, or about communication of a simple sharing or of a complex understanding of the situation by the therapist? Is it about the therapeutic stance of the therapist? Or, as Reed asks, is it about the presence of unconscious fantasy about the term that is reflected in the language used, and the relative interaction between affect and intellect? These issues are reflected in the variety of ways empathy is described in the literature. This existing ambiguity is accentuated by a lack of clear articulation in relation to psychoanalytic terminology.

Thus empathy remains a diffusely defined term in clinical theory, without the conceptual clarity of other psychoanalytic terms. What is the way out of this impasse? A possible line of solution is suggested in one work[13] — a comprehensive picture could be evolved by formulating a metapsychology of empathy from the genetic, dynamic, structural, economic and adaptive points of view. However, this task is hindered by a poor understanding of the role of unconscious, and by epistemological polemics which are accentuated by the language and troupes of psychoanalysis. It is no surprise then that in order to avoid some of this confusion, Kohut declined to attempt a description of empathy using the language of psychoanalysis. This task may, however, be made easier by an acknowledgement of the issues discussed in this chapter.

---

[13] T. Shapiro, "The Development and Distortions of Empathy", *Psychoanalytic Quarterly*, **43**(1)4-25, 1974.

3

Psychoanalytic Considerations Towards a Definition of Empathy

A. Specific Contributions Towards A Definition of Empathy

EMPATHY, as a framing concept for intersubjective experience, has gained an increasingly important profile within psychoanalytic literature. From its inception in 1932 to 1955, the *Psychoanalytic Quarterly* recorded only one citation on empathy. In contrast, from 1967 to 1980, empathy was referenced twenty-three times.[1] Its significance, therefore, can no longer be ignored or overlooked.

It goes without saying that there is no dearth of material on empathy in psychoanalysis, and numerous have been the contributions to the concept of empathy within psychoanalytic thought. These contributions have either focused on different aspects of the concept or, on occasion, attempted to develop comprehensive models of understanding. In order to understand current conceptions it will help to give a brief outline of individual contributor's thoughts. Freud, for example, mentioned the term briefly, though he wrote extensively on psychoanalytic technique. Reik and Fliess both attempted detailed theoretical formulations. Ferenczi wrote extensively on the clinical aspects of empathic practice. Kohut

---

[1] T. Shapiro, "Empathy: A Critical Re-evaluation", in *Empathy" I* (ed. Lichtenberg J. et al.), pp. 103-28.

and the post-Kohutians have interpreted the concept in a number of different ways. Schafer has emphasized that the developmental and structural aspects of the concept require further theoretical articulation. In the past twenty years a number of other writers have attempted to articulate even more salient features of the concept by deepening the experiential understanding or by de-coding the structure underlying the empathic experience.

Although there are certain recurring themes and concepts used in framing the term, generally, each contributor focused on different aspects of the term, thus making it difficult, at face value, to compare and contrast uses of the term. In common parlance, the term is used to denote a very different clinical phenomenon. I will concentrate more on metapsychological perspectives in the hope that these will shed light on the plurality of clinical meanings and frames also.

FREUD

Freud's contribution to the concept of empathy is best approached by placing it in a historical perspective. Freud was influenced by the works of Theodor Lipps. A copy of Lipps' *Aesthetic* (1903) had margin notes scribbled on its pages by Freud; "Komik and Humor" is footnoted in Freud's "Jokes and Their Relation to the Unconscious" and Freud mentions empathy in his work on group psychology.[2] Freud also mentions empathy in his work on group psychology. Lipps, as we said earlier, was a key figure in phenomenology and psychology, and his study on empathy was commented upon

---

[2] Sigmund Freud, *Jokes and Their Relation to the Unconscious (1905)* (standard edn.), London: Hogarth Press, 1960, p. 8; Sigmund Freud, "Group Psychology and the Analysis of the Ego", in *Complete Psychology Works of Sigmund Freud*, ed. and tr. J. Strachey (standard edn.), London: Hogarth Press, 1955, vol. 18, pp. 69-144.

by Edmund Husserl, the founder of modern phenomenology. Thus, it is possible that Freud was aware of the discussion surrounding the notion of empathy.

Further, at the time of formulating his thoughts on psychoanalytic technique, he was in close correspondence with two people who were writing extensively on the topic of empathy. Both Fliess and Ferenczi were proposing theories of technique which contrasted with Freud's austere "rule of abstinence". Freud had introduced the notion of "tact" into psychoanalysis in relation to the therapist's mode of listening. This was later developed into the notion of "evenly suspended attention" and was thought to facilitate an atmosphere conducive of free association. The idea was taken further by Fliess and Ferenczi. However, there were marked differences in their espoused therapeutic orientations. This was of concern to Freud; he wrote cautioning Ferenczi on the "subjective nature" of his work on empathy.[3] Just as the concept of empathy was subsumed by other terms within psychoanalysis, this pivotal influence of empathy from the field of phenomenological psychology was discussed and subsumed within philosophy and psychology, and only in the last thirty years has it been brought to the present level of interest within psychoanalysis by the proponents of Self-Psychology. It is also possible that the early interest in empathy was, at that time, incorporated by Freud into other terms relating to technique. Freud construed empathy as a special form of communication and wrote "that it plays the largest part in our understanding

---

[3] A. Rachman, "The Rule of Empathy: Sandor Ferenczi's Pioneering Contributions to the Empathic Method in Psychoanalysis", *American Academy of Psychoanalysis Journal*, **16**(1): 1-27, 1988; S. Ferenczi, "Introjection and Transference" (1909), in E. Jones (ed. and tr.) *First Contributions to Psychoanalysis*, New York: Brunner/Mazel, 1980.

of what is inherently foreign to our ego in other people".[4]

Thus, the place of empathy in knowing another's mental life is commented on largely in relation to individual and group analyses. It seems that the early focus of empathy within psychoanalysis was subsumed by a groundswell of developing ideas. It is possible that empathy, like the notion of countertransference, was viewed as a less-than-fitting subject for scientific study and, as a result, relegated to the background by the establishment of a body of thought which, in turn, inhibited all attempts to survive scientific scrutiny. This may have contributed to a split within the Freudian following and rejection of such early heretics as Fliess and Ferenczi, who were espousing theories of empathic technique very different from Freud's theory of technique.

This rather simplified analysis, however, does not do full justice to the complexity of events, which can only be commented upon retrospectively. There are a number of accounts of those early days of Freud and his followers.[5] The interpretations of Freud's comments on the concept of empathy vary from being thought of as extensive to being thought of as sparse.[6]

Agosta[7] suggests that because of its popular usage within aesthetics, Freud preferred to avoid using empathy in order to obviate confusion and possibly contamination with the non-

---

[4] Sigmund Freud, "Group Psychology and the Analysis of the Ego", in *Complete Psychology Works of Sigmund Freud,* ed. and tr. J. Strachey (standard edn.), London: Hogarth Press, 1955, vol. 18, pp. 69-144.

[5] Peter Gay, *Freud: A Life for Our Time*, London/New York: Norton, 1988; P. Roazen, *Freud and His Followers*, New York: New York University Press, 1984.

[6] G.H. Northrup, *Psychoanalytic Issues in the Theory of Empathy* (Dissertation), Michigan: University Microfilms International, 1986 (Microfiche).

[7] L. Agosta, "Empathy and Intersubjectivity", in *Empathy I* (ed. Lichtenberg J. et al.), pp. 43-62.

scientific terminology of aesthetics. In actual fact, the sparsity of the literal contribution will remain largely a matter of conjecture. Nevertheless, many of the other concepts pertaining to psychoanalytic technique as defined by Freud appear to be important for a definition of empathy.

Rather than interpret Freud's interest in the concept of empathy in psychoanalysis, it is preferable to consider the early contributions to psychoanalysis as a thought collective, within which different theoretical positions were taken, notably Freud, Reik, Fliess and Ferenczi. It is from this collective that various ideas emerged and underwent further development. Freud himself constantly revised his formulations over time, but he maintained a rationalistic perspective as his fundamental belief system — which in turn would determine not only how he would be listening, but also what kinds of data he would collect. This, of course, is a function of an individual's values, background philosophy and, to some extent, training. That is not to say that Freud was unempathic; it merely points to a different conceptual mode of being with another.

Comparing Husserl's method of phenomenological reduction or *epocé* to Freud's basic rule of free association, Margulies observes:

> Both techniques prepare the subject to put aside the usual biases to observation. Both investigators knew that it is in the nature of the mind to resist certain explorations. Their lives were similar in several other ways — they lived from the 1850s to 1930s, published their principal works, namely "The Interpretations of Dreams" and "Logical Investigations" in 1900, and both were students of Franz Brentano, a philosopher interested in the nature of the mind's constitution of reality. (Margulies 1984: 1026).[8]

[8] A. Margulies, "Towards Empathy: The Uses of Wonder", *American Journal of Psychiatry*, **141**(9): 1025-33, 1984.

In spite of the differences, both psychoanalysis and phenomenology, in their own ways, utilize similar methods of investigation: phenomenology as the study of intentional structure of conscious experiences (i.e. with respect to how the world is internally presented), and psychoanalysis with its emphasis on the semantics and structure of the unconscious. Both share the rule of suspending judgement ("bracketing") in order to let the "essence" of the phenomenon emerge. From this perspective, it is possible to see a similarity between the "evenly hovering attention" as advocated by Freud and the principles of phenomenological reduction developed by Husserl. Seen in this light, the austerity of Freud's rule of suspending attention from other thoughts extraneous to the therapeutic setting now takes on new meaning. By excluding possible contaminants of thought from the process of analysis, Freud was advocating a particular style of listening which constituted an aspect of "rule of abstinence". Whether this mode of listening and responding is empathic appears to have been interpreted differently by various writers.

However, Freud had qualms about the overly "subjective approach" advocated by Ferenczi. This, as Margulies attempts to show, was because of the method presupposed in arriving at an understanding of the unconscious without overt influences from the therapist's personality.[9] In becoming part of the analytic technique, this "rule of abstinence" perhaps prevented early discussion of terms such as empathy and countertransference. But it was Reik who attempted to deepen Freud's initial handling of the concept of empathy.

REIK

In 1937 Reik published a book entitled *Listening with the Third Ear*, commenting on the process of psychological conjecture

---

[9] A. Margulies, "Towards Empathy: The Uses of Wonder", *American Journal of Psychiatry*, **141**(9): 1025-33, 1984.

that is unique to the psychoanalytic process.[10] Reik's process bore similarities to the process outlined by Fliess in relation to empathy, which involved projection and introjection. The two respective processes were similar in the postulated stages, but they differed in the labels used. Although Reik allowed for the contributions from the therapist's personality towards understanding the patient, he still appeared tentative about the role of idiosyncratic, defensive or complementary responses on the part of the therapist. He developed the process in three stages.

Stage one, for Reik, was the process of observation of both conscious and unconscious thoughts by the analyst, wherein impulses similar to the patients are induced in the analyst. These affects then form the basis of a cognitive conjecture about the patient's state and simultaneously the affect is interpolated into the ego of the therapist.

Stage two was postulated as the stage of unconscious assimilation where there is an unconscious resonance within the conjecture about the affect. Unlike the sterility of tea being passed in and out, this description allowed for a contribution from the intra-psychic world of the therapist. Reik maintained that this process of knowing another was not based on identification, in contrast to Fliess's presupposition, but rather an affective response within the therapist.

Reik then postulated projection of this self-representation onto the patient, having taken care to state earlier that introjection was induced by the patient; hence nothing could be returned that was not characteristic of the patient in the first place. In this formulation of the process of understanding another the role of projection remained unclear, but it was nevertheless seen as being important for bringing to the conscious a vicarious experience of unconscious observations.

---

[10] T. Reik, *Listening with the Third Ear*, New York: E. Farrar Strauss, 1937.

The third stage related to the conscious assimilation of the conjecture. Thus Reik seemed to be proposing both a cognitive and an affective component to this process of knowing as well as an understanding of countertransference. However, the role of mental representation and object relations was neglected and the problems of semantics remained as it were hovering. Fliess, as already anticipated, in reacting to Reik's position took a somewhat variant approach.

FLIESS

R. Fliess examined the notion of empathy at great length.[11] In 1942, he presented a detailed formulation of the concept in a paper. However, the account he gave was obscure on a number of points, and the language used implied a mechanistic notion of empathy which was based on analogies to "tea tasting" and laws of bacteriology. Impressions of the other were thought to be transplanted within the recipient and returned without admixtures between host and parasite. There was a tacit alliance with drive theory; it was never explained what it is that is sampled of the other and so the role of the object representation is left unclear.

Although Fliess delineated four stages of empathy, he appears to have been describing two kinds of processes. The first is a "taking in" of an aspect as part of the patient (or of the other). Here the means of taking in are unclear, while terms such as incorporation, identification and introjection are used interchangeably. In the second process there follows a return to the patient of this very aspect, free of admixtures from the therapist. The nature of this aspect remains unclear;

---

[11] R. Fliess, "The Metapsychology of the Analyst", *Psychoanalytic Quarterly*, **11**: 211-27, 1942; R. Fliess, "Countertransference and Counteridentification", *Journal of the American Psychoanalytic Association*, **1**: 268-84, 1953.

one is left to surmise that it is either the mind, ego or instincts of the patient rather than a mental representation of these. The aspect of the patient that is internalized is then cognitively understood by means of a series of trial identifications with the therapist's own past experience. This presumably provides the therapist with an intellectual distance, without the experience of an affective resonance or immediacy that might otherwise prove to be harmful to the welfare of the therapist. In order to protect the therapist from this aspect of the patient taken in, Fliess stressed the urgency of returning to the patient this internalized aspect at the end of the session without unduly causing harm to the mental health of the therapist.

Within this framework, empathy remains a mechanistic process where the aspect of the other is internalized, assimilated, assessed and returned safely, free from admixtures or modifications by the therapist's own state. It is revealing that the metaphor from Virchow's bacteriology laboratory is utilized, as this seems to sum up the clinical precision with which Fliess viewed empathy.

The mechanism of empathy was thought to occur by a process of trial understanding based on the processes of introjection and projection, which however were not clearly articulated. It appears that some aspect of the patient is either internalized or that some aspect of the therapist is externalized, with a pre-eminent emphasis being placed on the identificatory process. Nevertheless, this unclear interchange between patient and therapist as proposed by Fliess reflects of the difficulties encountered in attempting to describe empathy in rigid psychoanalytic terms.

In short, Fliess' theory, although elaborate, suffers from a number of defects. The language of mechanisms carries with it an assumption of identifiable parts that are transferred from the patient to the therapist and returned to the patient to protect the therapist. The nature of these parts is not elucidated, neither is the role of representation explored. The insistence on clinical precision comes with an almost phobic denial of the role of the therapist's personality, and countertransference feelings in understanding another. The description is further complicated by an interchangeable use of terms, which tends to add to the lack of clarity in the account. By contrast, Ferenczi, as we shall now see, was much more careful and articulate in his modified approach.

FERENCZI

It is said that towards the end of his life, Ferenczi was working entirely within an empathic framework. Much of Ferenczi's ideas were confined to his diary and earlier in correspondence with Freud. Both sources remain largely untranslated.[12] However, Ferenczi did address himself to the issue of empathy and the broader issue of psychoanalytic technique in a number of articles. For instance, in "The Elasticity of Psychoanalytic Technique"[13] he attempted to develop the notion of "tact" as a means of reducing resistance to interpretations. A further component of his method involved an active awareness of non-verbal cues which he included in his observations as participant-observer. His description of this stance is that the therapist's mind "swings between empathy, self-observation and making judgements"(Ferenczi 1955: 96).[14]

Freud had introduced the notion of tact into psychoanalysis in relation to the therapist's mode of listening. This was later

---

[12] S. Ferenczi and O. Rank, *The Developmental Aims of Psychoanalysis*, USA: Nervous and Mental Disease Publishing Company, 1925.

[13] S. Ferenczi, "The Elasticity of Psychoanalytic Technique" (1928), in M. Balint (ed.), *Final Contributions to the Problems and Method of Psychoanalysis*, New York: Basic Books, 1955.

[14] S. Ferenczi, "The Elasticity of Psychoanalytic Technique" (1928), in M. Balint (ed.), *Final Contributions to the Problems and Method of Psychoanalysis*, New York: Basic Books, 1955.

developed into the notion of "evenly suspended attention" and was thought to facilitate an atmosphere conducive of free association. However, there were marked differences in their espoused therapeutic orientations. Freud, in a letter to Ferenczi, expressed his concern about the "subjective approach" suggested in relation to the therapeutic situation and the contribution and incorporation of countertransference into psychoanalytic technique.[15]

An analysis of Ferenczi's work reveals an emphasis on the inner psychic world of the analyst and on the ambience created by a deep sense of caring, such that the analysands feel comfortable enough to bypass pretensions and reveal the innermost core of their selves. Ferenczi felt that such a stance prevented further narcissistic injuries, and provided an opportunity for a real reparative experience leading to the possibility of the analysand being fully in the present reality without undue fixation and distortion from the past.

Ferenczi wrote on the impact of progressive relaxation of the mind, and the resulting possibility of "child talk" during therapy, in an attempt to bypass conscious critical faculties.[16] This was developed further in Sullivan's emphasis on making initial contact with the patient in a non-threatening manner and underscored in Kohut's suggestion of an empathic stance. This particular intentionality on the part of the therapist is also mentioned by Margulies for its importance in relation to the "initial encounter" with the patient. Such an approach may

---

[15] A. Rachman, "The Rule of Empathy: Sandor Ferenczi's Pioneering Contributions to the Empathic Method in Psychoanalysis", *American Academy of Psychoanalysis Journal*, **16**(1): 1-27, 1988.

[16] S. Ferenczi, "The Principle of Relaxation and Neo-Catharsis" (1930), in M. Balint (ed.), *Final Contributions to the Problems and Method of Psychoanalysis*, New York: Brunner/Mazel, 1912; repr. New York: Basic Books, 1955.

facilitate the development of transference, lessen the possibility of narcissistic injury and reduce undue resistance to the encounter. Rank later departed from Ferenczi and went on to develop the concept of short-term therapy.

In short, this empathic approach advocated by Ferenczi highlights the positive contributions that the therapist brings to the process in therapy. The strands of this line of thought can be seen in the work of Searles, Federn, Balint and other writers who have returned respectability to the notion of countertransference, albeit in relation to empathy. This in itself is a recent arrival in the field of psychoanalysis. And through his influence on Clara Thompsen and on Harry Stack Sullivan who referred Clara to Ferenczi for analysis, Ferenczi was to have profound impact on American psychoanalysis.

It may, then, come as a surprise to the critics and followers of Kohut that the present debate was foreshadowed by the work of that wildcard, Ferenczi, an early revisionist of the theory of psychoanalytic technique. However, Ferenczi's work on empathy was not developed extensively during his time and it is only now that the significance of his contributions to the present discussion is better appreciated.[17]

H.S. SULLIVAN

In the context of his discussion of the evolution of personality, Harry Stack Sullivan finished up with an elaboration of the concept of empathy. The reference to empathy appears in his writing as a description of an early bond between mother and child. This appears similar to the notion of synchronicity developed by latter-day infant research studies. This emotional

---

[17] S. Ferenczi, "Introjection and Transference" (1909), in E. Jones (ed. and tr.) *First Contributions to Psychoanalysis*, New York: Brunner/Mazel, 1980; S. Ferenczi, "On the Definition of Introjection", in M. Balint (ed.) *Final Contributions to the Problems and Methods of Psychoanalysi*, New York: Basic Books, 1955.

linkage between mother and infant is described by Sullivan as being responsible for the emotional contagion of the state of the mother to the child, and is seen as the vehicle for transmitting parental thought or emotion to the child.[18]

Later, Sullivan expanded the role of empathy as the vehicle for transmission of sex roles and cultural mores to the child, these being empathically apprehended by the child and transmitted by the parent of the same sex. This process was seen to result in greater antipathy to the parent of the same sex and a more prolonged idealization of the parent of the opposite sex. Thus, "empathy seems to function in childhood to produce a linkage of male to male and female to female". Empathy is postulated as an "extra link in the chain of processes" leading to identification with the parent of the same sex.[19]

Thus, in a developmental context, empathy is seen as the means of early transmission of thought and affect between the child and mother, and later as a socialization process and means by which gender identity is formed. This social psychology of empathy provides a basis for the recognition of similarities and differences, likes and dislikes, in later life. Though this early empathic apprehension between mother and child is seen as the basis for the development of empathy in later life, the developmental sequence is not clearly articulated.[20]

In any event, the early bond is seen by Sullivan as a

---

[18] P. Mullahy, *The Beginnings of Modem American Psychiatry*, Boston: Houghton Mifflin, 1973; H.S. Sullivan, "Personal Psychopathology", William Alanson White Psychiatric Foundation, Washington DC (unpublished MS), 1965 (quoted in Mullahy, 1973).

[19] H.S. Sullivan, "Personal Psychopathology", William Alanson White Psychiatric Foundation, Washington DC (unpublished MS), 1965 (quoted in Mullahy, 1973).

[20] H.S. Sullivan, "Socio-Psychiatric Research", *American Journal of Psychiatry*, **10**: 977-91, 1931.

prototype for later interpersonal relating. Indeed, Sullivan was responsible for giving rise to the early interpersonal school. In postulating the existence of a "tenderness theorem", it is unclear whether he felt that this was a biological given which leads to the subsequent engagement of the mother, initially, and later to the engagement of others. The description of the tenderness theorem is similar to Sullivan's description of emotional contagion and empathic bond.

Developmentally, the needs of the infant are thought to call forth a feeling of tenderness in the mother. The responsive actions of the mother are experienced as "tender behaviour", further inculcating a general need for tenderness such that an early need of the infant is expanded into a form of a dialogue between mother and child. Sullivan seems to imply that this need is built into the organism, and calls it an interpersonal need that is complemented and responded to in normal mothering. This reciprocal communication of tenderness, of "good feeling", is communicated, according to Sullivan, by means of empathy. Empathy, as such, then, is postulated as appearing in connection with anxiety between the ages of six and twenty months. However, in line with findings from infant research, it is possible that this need for tenderness is experienced at earlier stages. It seems, therefore, that Sullivan is postulating that a need for interpersonal relating emerges before — and may even be the prerequisite for — the structuring of experience. This "global matrix of what Sullivan refers to as tenderness is the first domain of human dialogue", (Mullahy 1973: 344, 348; Sullivan 1931)[21]

Bromberg, discussing Sullivan's ideas, suggests that it is on this background experience of tenderness that later anxiety-

---

[21] P. Mullahy, *The Beginnings of Modem American Psychiatry*, Boston: Houghton Mifflin, 1973; H.S. Sullivan, *The Interpersonal Theory of Psychiatry*, ed H.S. Perry and Gawel, New York: Norton, 1953.

organized personifications emerge. Mental processes develop as a continuum to interpersonal field process, and the representational world of the infant moves from an undifferentiated "interpersonal organization through a socialized process of gradually differentiated but egocentric organization (parataxic) to conceptual representation based on consensual validation (syntaxic)"(Bromberg 1980: 231).[22] Thus, early interpersonal experiences exist before self-and-other differences emerge in a state of empathic oneness. This formulation appears similar to the concept of narcissistic fusion proposed by Klein. However, Sullivan sees this early prototypic experience of tenderness as a prerequisite to the developmental socialization of empathy, whereas Klein focuses on an understanding of projective and introjective mechanisms.

In many ways, Sullivan's contribution to the topic seems an early forerunner of developmental studies on empathy. The metaphor of the parent–child bond is used to describe the roles and function of empathy as well as the therapeutic implications of an empathic stance. Meanwhile, a quite different interpretation of empathy evolved under the impetus of Heinz Kohut.

KOHUT

The writings of Kohut have drawn attention to the notion of empathy within psychoanalytic work. In the past thirty years the tenants of Self-Psychology have been expanded by Kohut and his followers. In an early paper in 1959, namely, "Introspection, Empathy and Psychoanalysis", Kohut drew attention to the central role of empathy in psychoanalysis.[23]

---

[22] P.M. Bromberg, "Empathy, Anxiety and Reality: A View from the Bridge", *Contemporary Psychoanalysis*, **16**(2): 223-36, 1980.

[23] Heinz Kohut, "Introspection, Empathy, and Psychoanlysis: An Examination of the Relationship Between Mode of Observation and Theory", *Journal of American Psychoanal. Association*, **7**: 459-83, 1959.

Since then further work on Self-Psychology has drawn much attention. Critics and commentators have either seen these developments as different from mainstream psychoanalysis or as new developments within psychoanalysis. This controversy is reflected in the discussion of empathy within the psychoanalytic literature. While it is claimed on the one hand that it is no different to other modes of listening and relating within psychoanalysis, it is generally acknowledged that, when working with severe personality disordered patients, the use of an empathic stance is quite novel.[24]

In a paper written prior to his death, "Introspection, Empathy and the Semi-Circle of Mental Health",[25] Kohut addressed the issues raised in the ensuing years and restated his thoughts on empathy, calling the clinical role of empathy the "low road" and the epistemological "the high road". In this paper he commented on the clinical functions of empathy, but more importantly, placed empathy within a larger discourse on epistemological differences between subject and object.

In clinical terms, Kohut defines empathy as a stance adopted by the therapist, wherein a value-free mode of perception is adopted towards the patient. While this experience-near mode of perception is also a means of information gathering, it also engenders a powerful emotional bond within the therapeutic dyad. Thus Kohut defined empathy as an affective in-tuneness as well as a cognitive information gathering and processing. This clinical stance allows for the uncovering and recovery of early self-object

---

[24] R.S. Wallerstein, "Self-Psychology and Classical Psychoanalytic Psychology: The Nature of Their Relationship", *Psychoanalysis and Contemporary Thought*, **6**: 4, 1983.

[25] Heinz Kohut, "Introspection, Empathy and the Semicircle of Mental Health", *International Journal of Psycho-Analysis*, **63**: 395-408, 1982.

transferences within the setting of a therapeutic relationship. Thus, empathy aids in the elucidation of the interpersonal elements of both the real and transference relationship.

In proposing a metapsychology of empathy, Kohut instigated an examination of empathy as a means of knowing another. In doing so he appeared to be proposing a move in the direction of a metapsychology, not so much based on drive theory but on an understanding of the self. While not negating the value of drive theory, he appeared to postulate that the core self is accessible, not so much by interpretive confrontation but by empathic listening. Fundamentally, Kohut's view differs from that of Freud. In moving away from a metapsychology of drives, Kohut places the study of human beings within an intersubjective realm, whereby, self-identity is formed on the basis of continuous experiences of others, internalized as self-objects. The similarities of Self-Psychology to object relations theory and interpersonal psychoanalysis are beyond the confines of this work.

Criticisms of Kohut's emphasis on empathy and introspection refer to the similarities of these concepts to other psychoanalytic concepts such as the therapeutic alliance, interpretation and cure. It is apparent that the issue of empathy raises questions pertinent to the theory and practice of psychoanalysis.[26] While classical psychoanalysis was concerned with understanding the mechanisms of the intrasubjective world, the contextual study of self and empathy involve an exploration of the intersubjective realms and the meaning that this holds for the individual. After Kohut, several contemporary writers have tended to pursue rather different directions in emphasizing one or the other facet of empathy

---

[26] R.S. Wallerstein, "Self-Psychology and Classical Psychoanalytic Psychology: The Nature of Their Relationship", *Psychoanalysis and Contemporary Thought*, **6**: 4, 1983.

enunciated by the "masters" of the proliferating psychoanalytic schools. We shall consider a few such positions, finishing with the significant contribution of Shapiro in this regard.

SCHAFER

Schafer develops the concept of generative empathy. He uses the term in an Ericksonian sense to denote a process that promotes growth in the subject, object and the relationship between them.[27] He describes empathy as an inner experience involving both cognitive and affective components. As such it involves experiencing the feelings of another, but there is recognition of the other's separateness and individuality.

To describe the mechanisms of the process, Schafer places the process within the workings of the work ego, wherein an adaptive regression is integrated with the rest of the ego. An analogy is drawn with Kris's concept of regression within the service of the ego, such that empathy is seen as creative process whereby the free play of primary process is allowed a place and is integrated into conscious experience.

GREENSON

In 1960, Ralph Greenson published a paper "Empathy and Its Vicissitudes",[28] in which he describes the pathology of empathy as inhibition or loss of control of empathy. He also differentiates empathy from sympathy on the basis of intent. Sympathy involves condolence and pity whereas empathy is sharing the quality of the other's experience and impulses, which, in turn, leads to a better understanding of the other. A distinction between empathy and intuition is also made on the basis of intuition pertaining to the realm of ideas.

---

[27] R. Schafer, "Generative Empathy in the Treatment Situation", *Psychoanalytic Quarterly*, **28**: 342-73, 1959.

[28] R. Greenson, "Empathy and Its Vicissitudes", *International Journal of Psychoanalysis*, **41**: 418-28, 1960.

OLDEN

Olden defines empathy as a capacity of the ego to instinctively and intuitively think as the object does, and it is possibly an end-product of sublimation of the mother–child unity, somewhat akin to a residual umbilical cord.[29]

BERES AND ARLOW

In 1974, Beres and Arlow published a paper "Fantasy and Identification in Empathy", developing an earlier work on the role of empathy in psychotherapy.[30] Identification is emphasized as being transient and multiple other functions are involved in the empathic process other than an immediate affective response. Identification is followed by a separation process. The picture is further complicated by the possibility of identification with other than the patient's affects, i.e. resistances, thus highlighting the possible sources of misunderstanding with an empathic stance.

BASCH

M.F. Basch bases his theory of empathy on Silvan Tomkins' theory of affects.[31] Tomkins postulated nine inherited, universal identifiable patterns present at birth with which the human autonomic nervous system responds to stimulation. These are stress, interest, joy, distress, anger, fear, shame, contempt and disgust. These basic affects are seen as biological programmes in the autonomic nervous system. These nine patterns provide

[29] C. Olden, "On Adult Empathy with Children", *Psychoanalytic Study of the Child*, **8**: 110-26, 1953.

[30] D. Beres, "The Role of Empathy in Psychotherapy and Psychoanalysis", *Journal of the Hillside Hospital*, **17**: 362-69, 1968; D. Beres and J.A. Arlow, "Fantasy and Identification in Empathy", *Psychoanalytic Quarterly*, **43**: 155-81, 1974.

[31] M.F. Basch, "Empathic Understanding: A Review of the Concept and Some Theoretical Considerations", *Journal of the American Psychoanalytic Association*, **31**: 101-26, 1983.

a basis for the affective resonance that forms the basis of the affective experience. Affect by this account is always unconscious since it is a programmed autonomic response. Basch then goes on to conceptualize a progressive development from affects, feelings and emotions to the stage of empathic understanding. These stages do not replace each other but add a new dimension to affective communication, integrating what has gone before. Basch postulates that between eighteen and twenty-four months of age, the conscious awareness of an affective event becomes possible as a feeling.

Basch however also postulates that emotions are much more complex states in which several feelings are experienced together with autonomic and cognitive responses, which may result in action. Affective sensitivity has a variety of goals, empathic understanding being only one of them. Thus, selfish use or inappropriate use of the empathic sense is possible. This description of the potentiality of misuse of an empathic sense has some points of similarity to the definition of an altruistic defence as defined by Anna Freud.

Basch's value-free formulation differs from that of Schafer who implies an altruistic component to empathy, though he repeats a point made by Schäfer: empathy is a complex process. In contrast, Basch differentiates mature empathy, defined as being value-laden and caring, from a more primitive valueless state.

NORTHRUP

Northrup, who we mentioned in the preceding chapters, distinguishes two approaches towards an empathic apprehension of another — the introspective and the extrospective.[32] The introspective relates to the inner world

[32] G.H. Northrup, *Psychoanalytic Issues in the Theory of Empathy* (Dissertation), Michigan: University Microfilms International, 1986 (Microfiche).

of the therapist and is purely a subjective mode. The extrospective mode is analogous to the methods of natural science and relates to the knowledge of an objective reality. Although psychoanalytic practice is described as utilizing both approaches, claims for the superiority of one approach above the other are not infrequent in the literature. Both approaches are inferences and they approach the thing in itself from different perspectives and, perhaps, reveal different aspects of reality.

The extrospective observer, as defined by Northrup, bases his or her findings on sense data. Claims about the theory-ladenness of sense data are documented in the literature.[33] However, classically, within this perspective, the therapist distinguishes between the expressions of the patient and the therapist's working model of the patient's reality, in keeping with a distinction between subjective and objective realities. The secondary-process inferences are supposedly kept separate from other forms of response from the therapist.

In drawing a contrast, introspection is described as the observing function of self-reflective states. What is observed is the psychic life of the therapist's "conscious, unconscious, thoughts, feelings, desires, memories, bodily sensations, fantasies, etc.".[34] These subjective responses can either be excluded as contaminants to the therapeutic or utilized to provide further understanding. It is evident that in the therapeutic situation, both forms of information, gathering are utilized. An entirely introspective, solipsistic approach

---

[33] T.S Kuhn, *The Structure of Scientific Revolution* (rev. edn), Chicago: University of Chicago Press, 1962; Adolf Grunbaum, *The Foundations of Psychoanalysis: A Philosophical Critique*, Berkeley: University of California Press, 1984.

[34] G.H. Northrup, *Psychoanalytic Issues in the Theory of Empathy* (Dissertation), Michigan: University Microfilms International, 1986 (Microfiche).

would ignore the reality of the other and, on the other hand, the perception of the observer is always tainted by subjectivity.

The mechanistic analogy described by Northrup is complicated further by the activity that both processes occur simultaneously at all levels of awareness. If, for instance, the empathic appraisal is made "in the twinning of a glance" (to borrow a metaphor from poetry), it is difficult to know what perspective, at the exclusion of the other, is being utilized at that moment. This presupposes only the empathic capacity of the therapist. If, for instance, the patient is also credited with empathic ability, then the field of interaction becomes even more complex, somewhat reminiscent of the Jamesian "blooming, buzzing confusion". Thus, it appears that not only it is difficult to define the process of empathy but, as Northrup discusses, mechanical reification can lead to a distorted notion of the term.

Along with a historical examination of the notion of empathy, Northrup defines the notion of empathic projection and identification on the basis of introjection. These concepts will be discussed later in relation to the notions of projection and introjection.

SHAPIRO

In two thoughtful and critical reviews, Shapiro outlines the difficulty with simplistic notions of complex phenomena.[35] In reviewing the literature he identifies some of the features not commonly addressed, but which are of paramount importance in understanding empathy. In his analysis of the literature, he raises epistemological issues previously discussed in this thesis. The issues raised relate to: the question of subject–object

[35] T. Shapiro, "The Development and Distortions of Empathy", *Psychoanalytic Quarterly*, **43**(1)4-25, 1974; T. Shapiro, "Empathy: A Critical Re-evaluation", in *Empathy" I* (ed. Lichtenberg J. et al.), pp. 103-28.

distance; the assumption that the affect empathized with is the same as that experienced; the difference between empathy as an affect and ego state; the difference between affect and ideation; and the insufficient examination of dynamic and structural components, rather than a reliance on the phenomenal descriptive process.

Thus, in proposing a need to examine the dynamic, structural and adaptive mechanisms composing the experience of empathy, Shapiro suggests a need for the examination of the distortions of the normal development of empathy that may manifest as obstacles in conducting therapy in a number of identifiable ways. The following examples of possible distortions are given: the confusion of empathy with countertransference reactions or an altruistic defence; an overemphasis on affect at the cost of examining other non-affective but equally relevant experiences; a defence against confronting interpretive work and a more precise definition of the patient's conflict, which may result in an over-idealization and mutual gratification and, thus, a resulting over-emphasis on the real relationship rather than on transference analysis. Shapiro's comments serve as a reminder of the possible inappropriate uses of empathy and, thus, the need for a better elucidation of the concept.

MID-SUMMARY

While examining the specific contributions towards attempts at defining the term empathy, a number of perspectives emerge. Sullivan, in describing the tenderness theorem, placed the origins of empathy within the mother–child relationship. Likewise, Olden invoked the notion of the umbilical cord as a metaphor for empathy. Fliess and Reik took great pains to describe the mechanisms of the process within the therapeutic setting. Although Fliess advocated a clinical distance, Reik made attempts to understand the role of countertransference within the therapeutic setting. Much later, Shapiro also advocated the careful development of an understanding of the mechanisms of empathy in structural terms and Schafer placed the capacity for empathy within the mechanisms of the work ego. The work of Basch is aimed at an understanding of empathy within the context of autonomic reactivity and affect.

The functions of empathy were developed by Sullivan in relation to a socialization role of empathy as well as a role in personality development, while Kohut expanded on the function of empathy within the therapeutic setting. The epistemological status in relation to subject–object differences was originally commented on by Freud, then commented on extensively by Kohut and further developed by Northrup. Thus, the study of these commentaries on empathy sheds light on the aetiology, descriptive mechanisms, function and epistemological status of empathy.

B. Empathy in Relationship to Other Psychotherapeutic Categories

The technique of psychoanalysis, as initially elucidated by Freud, has undergone a number of revisions. Terms such as identification, ego and introjection, can only be understood within a historical–contextual framework. Sandler aptly puts it:

> The search for precise definitions has led to difficulties and inconsistencies in the various presentations of psychoanalytic concepts in the increasingly available psychoanalytic glossaries and dictionaries. — Sandler et al.1973: 13.[36]

Two observations are apposite here.

First, various authors have defined the component parts

[36] J. Sandler, C. Dare and A. Holder, *The Patient and the Analyst*, London: Maresfield Library, 1973.

of the relationship between therapist and patient alike. Most therapists differentiate between re-lived transference and the real reparative relationship between therapist and patient.

Second, whereas the analysis of transference was the mainstay of treatment of neurotic patients in the past, in more recent times psychoanalytic work has concentrated on an understanding of the real reparative object relationship as, for instance, represented in the works of Frieda Fromm Reichmann, Paul Federn, Harold Searles, Sullivan, Winnicott, and Kohut. The concept of empathy has relevance for, and appears to be defined by, these existing terms describing the therapeutic relationship. Often the relationship between these terms is poorly articulated and the notion of empathy is used in a number of different ways, as has been described in the preceding section.

THERAPEUTIC STANCE

In considering the therapeutic stance, a number of writers have placed emphasis on the therapist's orientation towards the patient. Freud advocated the use of free-floating attention and tact. This can be described as being similar to the phenomenological approach, according to which what is familiar to the mind is "bracketed" in order to better grasp the undisclosed phenomenon. Ferenczi postulated an empathic stance and focused on the oscillation of the therapist's mind between unconscious fantasy and logical thinking. Reik described a special way of thinking whereby an unconscious thought leads to the formulation of a conjecture, which, in turn, is subject to more rational and conscious elucidation. Otto Isakower (1889–1972) introduced the notion of the "analysing instrument", a non-critical concentration on the communicative and perceptual field.[37]

---

[37] G.H. Northrup, *Psychoanalytic Issues in the Theory of Empathy* (Dissertation), Michigan: University Microfilms International, 1986 (Microfiche).

Similarly, Bion attempted to elucidate the changes in perception of the therapist's mindset in the context of attention, which is free of memory or desire. Kohut placed emphasis on the non-judgemental anthropological stance of the analyst, which to him has the function of information-gathering as well as being therapeutic and minimizing the possibility of perpetrating further narcissistic injury. Thus the notion of "vicarious introspection" introduced by Kohut has epistemo-logical and therapeutic significance. The stance includes the therapist's particular orientation — be that an emphasis on understanding transference, the working alliance, the real relationship, focus on phenomenological reduction, attention to fantasy imagination and primary processes or logical secondary idiographic methods of thinking — and this will naturally depend on training and personality of the therapist.

Perhaps, then, as Northrup suggests, empathy functions as a supra-ordinate, overarching stance that exists irrespective of a conscious espousal, and it deepens whatever perspective the therapist at given moment, might be consciously using. As such the empathic stance does not stand outside or separate from existing techniques, but can serve to deepen our knowledge of existing practices. This may account for the finding that although empathy and therapeutic stance are often linked in the literature, these terms are poorly articulated in relation to each other.

REAL RELATIONSHIP

The real relationship refers to the reality-orientated, non-transferential aspects of the therapeutic relationship in contrast to the transference relationship, which is genuine but involves the working through of past experiences, and in contrast to the working alliance which is seen as real and in the present but a product of the unequal therapeutic situation.[38] The real

---

[38] J. Sandler, C. Dare and A. Holder, *The Patient and the Analyst*, London: Maresfield Library, 1973.

relationship is expressed by the gestalt therapists as a direct experience of the other person. Kohler states that this perceptual process is not based on inference or analogy as in trial identification, physical or affect contagion, but purely on a perception of the other. Ontologically, this stance appears similar to the Heideggerian notion of "unconcealment" (*aletheia*) where the other is not reduced to a series of self-reflections or to general psychic principles, but is acknowledged as being different, as well as similar, to oneself.

According to Rogers, accurate empathic perception of the other depends on the therapist's genuineness, on an unconditional positive regard for the client, and on the therapist's sensitive and accurate empathic understanding of the client's feelings and personal language. These attitudes are effectively communicated to the patient in a client-centred approach. Rogers views empathy as not just an anthropological data-gathering exercise, as defined by Kohut, nor as simply testing a readiness for a curative explanation, but more as a means of communicating an in-tune-ness.

In a review of the existentialist and interpersonal approaches to therapy, Margulies and Havens explore the reality orientation of these two approaches.[39] The existentialists focus on the whole person's experience of being-in-the-world. An undue preoccupation with theory or pathology is seen as a distraction to also being aware of the present actual relationship. Empathic contact is established by putting aside "expectations, pre-judgements and objectification of the patient and attempting to meet the patient where he is".[40] This setting

---

[39] A. Margulies and L.L. Havens, "The Initial Encounter: What to Do First?", *American Journal of Psychiatry*, **138**(4): 421-28, 1981.

[40] A. Margulies, "Towards Empathy: The Uses of Wonder", *American Journal of Psychiatry*, **141**(9): 1025-33, 1984.

aside of expectations is also advocated, by phenomenologists, towards internal or external phenomena.

May, Ellenberger, Freud and Greenson are cited as being aware of this immediacy of contact by Margulies. Buber and Rogers advocate, and indeed exemplify, an empathic style of therapy whereby the immediacy of contact leads to innovative insights on the part of both therapist and patient. They state that it is this phase of initial empathy or compassion, whether it be existential or interpersonal, that leads to a successful working through in therapy, especially with patients who cannot benefit from classical analytic methods that utilize transference alone. In the descriptions cited, although empathy plays a large part in the perceptive stance of the therapist, it is not often articulated further. Although empathy appears similar to the notion of affective resonance, there appears to be ontological differences in espousing a particular stance.

IDENTIFICATION

The term "identification" is used often in relation to empathy. For example Fliess saw trial identification as being a basis of empathy and what is presupposed here is a clearly articulated definition of identification. However, in reviewing the literature on identification, what becomes apparent is that, like a number of psychoanalytic terms, the ambiguities present in the initial usage have persisted alongside later developmental changes in the concept. As discussed earlier, in the case of empathy, the historical, semantic and epistemological confusions contribute to the difficulty in arriving at an operational definition of the term.

Historically, identification derives from the Latin word *idem*, meaning "the same", although the concept has been around for much longer.[41] Like the term empathy, identification

[41] G. Halasz, "Identification: Theoretical and Clinical Aspects", Papers of the Freudian School of Melbourne, ed. Oscar Zentner, 1988.

was used by Aristotle to connote an animistic projection, the notion of man as a *mimeticon zoon* (translated as "an animal that identifies with another"), and it thus predates current psychoanalytic discussions.

In a comprehensive account of the evolving psychoanalytic theory of identification, Compton[42] states that "the concept of identification, as Freud left it in 1938, was far different in scope from what it had been in his work before 1921". Initially described as a mechanism responsible for certain kinds of psychopathology, it was later used in relation to psychic structure and seen as being important for normal development. Freud introduced the concept in "The Interpretation of Dreams" and later elaborated on it in "Group Psychology and the Analysis of the Ego".

Described initially in relation to the oral phase, identification was later connected to an earlier, primary phase of identification, prior to the phase of object relating. Thus a developmental notion was introduced. Structurally, the idea of identification was situated within the psychic structure, i.e. placement within the ego, ego-ideal, or superego determined its effects. Freud also felt that a variety of affective overtones were associated in relation to oedipal and pre-oedipal identifications and, in a way, related to "object" loss and/or love. A number of articles have traced the origins and developments of this concept within Freud's writings.[43]

---

[42] A. Compton, "The Concept of Identification in the Work of Freud, Ferenczi, and Abraham: A Review and Commentary", *Psychoanalytic Quarterly*, **44**: 200-233, 1985.

[43] G. Halasz, "Identification: Theoretical and Clinical Aspects", Papers of the Freudian School of Melbourne, ed. Oscar Zentner, 1988; A. Compton, "The Concept of Identification in the Work of Freud, Ferenczi, and Abraham: A Review and Commentary", *Psychoanalytic Quarterly*, **44**: 200-233, 1985; L.M. Birchhead, "Identification as an Appropriate Component of Therapeutic Growth and Development", *Issues in Mental Health Nursing*, **6**(1-

→

Halasz[44] traces the temporal and semantic shifts in defining the concept of identification and suggests that infant research studies will open up the possibility of studying affect identification between mother and child as the basis of reciprocity and mutual attunement. As discussed earlier, the developmental studies of empathy may provide different metaphors for describing the relationship between self and other. Thus, both the terms, empathy and identification, relate to the issues of defining the similarities and differences between self and other, the process of perception, aspects of mental representation and object relations, implications for normal and pathological personality development, and their respective roles in the therapeutic process.

Halasz, in discussing the semantic confusion surrounding the term identification, states that

> whilst all the terms describe similar processes of "taking in" . . . some inherently emphasize the earlier "somatic" aspects of physical taking in, while others refer to the more psychical equivalents of "mental" ingestion . . . In current practice these words do have overlapping meanings and are sometimes used interchangeably.[45] — Halasz 1988: 62.

Similarly, in defining the interchangeable use of words to define empathy, the inherent epistemological confusions are compounded.

→ 2): 73-88, 1984; W.W. Meissner, "Notes on Identification, III: The Concept of Identification", *Psychoanalytic Quarterly*, **41**(2): 224-60, 1974; J. Laplanche and J.B. Pontalis, *The Language of Psychoanalysis*, London: The Hogarth Press and The Institute of Psychoanalysis, 1985.

[44] G. Halasz, "Identification: Theoretical and Clinical Aspects", Papers of the Freudian School of Melbourne, ed. Oscar Zentner, 1988.

[45] G. Halasz, "Identification: Theoretical and Clinical Aspects", Papers of the Freudian School of Melbourne, ed. Oscar Zentner, 1988.

COUNTERTRANSFERENCE

Not unlike the term empathy, little direct reference to countertransference is present in Freud's work, possibly due to his early belief that it was counter-productive to therapeutic work.[46] Furthermore, there has been increasing awareness of the phenomenon in the past thirty years, as evidenced by the growing body of work in the area. Comprehensive reviews of the literature by Laplanche and Pontalis, Sandler et al. and Tyson trace the historical profile and conceptual difficulties in defining the term.[47] Although countertransference is mentioned in relation to empathy, there is little detailed analysis of the possible relationship. This may be due to the relative lack of clarity in the definition of both concepts.

Initially, Freud defined countertransference as the patient's influence on the unconscious feelings of the analyst. He advocated initially self analysis and, later, a training analysis to examine these influences. In his second and direct reference to countertransference, Freud defined the term as an unconscious reaction to the patient's transference and, as such, a breakdown of the requisite analytic neutrality and an obstacle to further analytic work. This has come to be regarded as the classical position and precludes other reactions of the analyst to the patient such as the analyst's transference to the patient.

In a detailed review, Tyson explores the ways in which

---

[46] L.M. Birchhead, "Identification as an Appropriate Component of Therapeutic Growth and Development", *Issues in Mental Health Nursing*, **6**(1-2): 73-88, 1984.

[47] J. Sandler, C. Dare and A. Holder, *The Patient and the Analyst*, London: Maresfield Library, 1973;J. Laplanche and J.B. Pontalis, *The Language of Psychoanalysis*, London: The Hogarth Press and The Institute of Psychoanalysis, 1985; R.L. Tyson, "Countertransference Evolution in Theory and practice", *Journal of the American Psychoanalytic Association*, **34**(2): 251-74, 1986.

the notion has been expanded since its inception and lists six areas for examination, i.e. the inclusion of conscious as well as unconscious responses of the analyst; an expansion of the concept to include transference as well as the total responses of the therapist; an improved understanding of the mechanisms that underlie countertransference reactions; the ability to recognize and deal with the responses evoked in the therapist; and, finally, whether the analyst's responses are aids or hindrances to treatment.

These same issues appear in the literature in relation to the role and function of empathy and were discussed earlier in relation to an epistemological definition of empathy. Although the interrelationship between the concepts is not clearly articulated, both concepts relate to the distinctions previously discussed in relation to self and object/other perception and distinction. These distinctions between therapist and other, and therapist neutrality appear to be more readily challenged by work with the grossly disturbed as described by Little, Searles, Winnicott and others, necessitating a discussion of empathy, projective identification and countertransference in relation to severely disturbed patients.[48]

The mechanisms underlying countertransference have been described in a number of ways. Sandler defines the concept in object relations terms, and distinguishes "useful" responses which may be used to deepen insight within the analytic situation. Fliess[49] defined the "work ego" as the critical aspect of the therapist's working personality, and empathy based on

---

[48] H.F. Searles, "The Self in the Countertransference", *Issues in Ego Psychology*, **2**(2): 49-56, 1979; D.W. Winnicott, "Hate in the Countertransference", *International Journal of Psychoanalysis*, **30**: 69-74, 1949; M. Little, "Countertransferance and the Patient's Response to It", *International Journal of Psychoanalysis*, **32**: 2-40, 1951.

[49] R. Fliess, "The Metapsychology of the Analyst", *Psychoanalytic Quarterly*, **11**: 211-27, 1942.

trial identification as the basis of the analytic process. Schafer has later added the notion of the "work superego" and the analyst's second self. Racker has incorporated and enlarged on Deutsch's notion of complementary identification as distinct from concordant identification.[50]

Grinberg described projective counter-identification as the use of projective identification on the part of the analyst.[51] However, as Tyson points out,

> there are difficulties in distinguishing between what is required of the analyst for his therapeutic work and what he offers as self-justification for his actions.[52]

The difficulties encountered by prescribed definitions of empathy, regression and countertransference are highlighted by the clinical finding that what is described as empathy for one person may be countertransference for another. These clinical uncertainties are further complicated by the semantic and epistemological confusion in the definition of these terms.

The utility and clinical value of countertransference are widely debated in the literature. In the classical view, it is seen as a hindrance to the process of analysis. We shall look at some examples now:

- Heimann, in his effort to expand the concept, saw countertransference as a possible source of insight but was cautious about the possible limitations of its use.[53]

---

[50] H. Racker, "The Meanings and Uses of Countertransference", *Psychoanalytic Quarterly*, **26**: 303-57, 1957.

[51] L. Grigberg, "On a Specific Aspect of Countertransference Due to the Patient's Projective Identification", *International Journal of Psychoanalysis*, **43**: 436-40, 1962.

[52] R.L. Tyson, "Countertransference Evolution in Theory and practice", *Journal of the American Psychoanalytic Association*, **34**(2): 251-74, 1986.

[53] P. Heimann, "On Countertransference", *International Journal of Psychoanalysis*, **31**: 81-84, 1950.

- Mashud Khan defines countertransference as "a clinical instrument of perception" that allows insight into the inner world of the patient and a use of the therapist's creative and imaginative abilities towards this aim.[54]
- Reich sees countertransference reactions arising in the context of a block in the therapist's empathic function and that not all the possible responses are induced by the patient.[55]
- J. McDougal takes the position that the analyst's reactions can be indicative of primitive pre-verbal and pre-symbolic communications from the patient.[56]
- Michel deM' Uzan describes paradoxical thinking and introjective identification as a further form of primitive communication.
- M.J. Tansey and W.F.H. Burke look upon countertransference as a supraordinate term, encompassing projective identification and empathy.[57]

Similar accounts of the limitations and usefulness of empathy

---

[54] M.M.R. Khan, *The Privacy of the Self*, New York: International University Press, 1974.

[55] A. Reich, "On Countertransference", *International Journal of Psychoanalysis*, **32**: 25-31, 1951; A. Reich, "Further Remarks on Countertransference", *International Journal of Psychoanalysis*, **41**: 389-95, 1960; A. Reich, "Empathy and Countertransference", in Annie Reich, *Psychoanalytic Contributions*, New York: International Universities Press, 1966.

[56] J. McDougal, "Countertransference and Primitive Communication", in *Plea for a Measure of Insanity*, New York: International Universities Press, 1978.

[57] M.J. Tansey and W.F.H. Burke, *Understanding Countertransference from Projective Identification to Empathy*, Hillsdale, NJ: The Analytic Press, 1989.

in the therapeutic process have been discussed earlier.[58] At present it appears that further delineation between the concepts is necessary to provide a functional and theoretical distinction between empathy and counter-transference, as well as an understanding of their common links.

PROJECTION AND INTROJECTION

Both Fliess and Reik use the terms "introjection" and "projection" in their respective definitions of empathy. Although differing in their use of the terms both felt that projection followed introjection and was a means of returning to the patient aspects that could be dangerous to the health of the therapist. However, Reik was prepared to concede that the therapist's personality could contribute to this process while for Fliess, projection was a means of terminating trial identification. In distinction to Fliess's view, Knight placed projection as occurring prior to introjection and he was at pains to make a distinction between identifying with an object and identifying an object with oneself.

First, with the growing move to recognize enabling and adaptive aspects of the defensive function, Northrup proposes an alternative term, namely, "empathic projection", in order to differentiate between adaptive and pathological functions of projection. "Empathic projection" is defined as

> an intra-psychic process occurring during a state of adaptive regression in which a conscious or unconscious idea, affect, motive, fantasy or self-representation . . . object representation or introjects . . . of the therapist are represented as the patient's . . . in a temporary and tentative way . . . the origin of the projected material and the projective process

---

[58] T. Shapiro, "The Development and Distortions of Empathy", *Psychoanalytic Quarter*ly, **43**(1)4-25, 1974; T. Shapiro, "Empathy: A Critical Re-evaluation", in *Empathy" I* (ed. Lichtenberg J. et al.), pp. 103-28.

> itself are either immediately, or upon, reflection recognizable to the therapist.

This non-defensive use of the process of projection is an aspect of aesthetic appreciation and creativity. However, what is not clear is first to what degree experiences outside the experience of the therapist are amenable to empathic projection.

Second, empathic projection places the focus of activity within the subjectivity of the therapist, and thus runs the risk of becoming solipsistic rather than an incorporation of both introspective and sense data as proposed earlier by Northrup.

Third, this notion of empathic projection remains poorly articulated in relation to the concepts of introjection, incorporation, identification and projective identification. Further elucidation may lead to mechanical reification of fluid dynamic processes and thus further semantic splitting, or else lead to a clearer articulation of the notion of empathy and other related terms would be needed.

Similarly, the concept of introjection remains poorly differentiated from other psychoanalytic concepts, such as identification, incorporation and object representation. Ferenczi, who introduced the term, viewed it as an object-hunger associated with libidinal impulses. Freud defined it as the relation of a living being to the object that it desires. Klein took these ideas and defined the processes as literal whereas Lacan initially subscribed more to an introjection of images initially and later a "scripting" of the self by the effects of language, leading on to a layering of representations. The relationship between early image formation, imagination and language is a complex one and leads to a complex representation of the world and self (Ragland-Sullivan).

Northrup defines introjection as a kind of transitional representation that is not quite object-representation or identification, i.e. neither self or object-other. Stated differently, this position is not identification or a purely differentiated observational posture. Northrup postulates that these introjects are modelled on early object relations associated with the superego. As such, empathic introjection is seen as akin to placing the patient in the role of ego ideal with which brief identifications may occur. Without going into semantic debates, this argument presupposes a clear notion of superego. Furthermore, it remains incompletely articulated to other concepts such as empathic projection, incorporation, identification and projective identification.

PROJECTIVE IDENTIFICATION

A review of the literature shows that projective identification has been described in a number of ways. Initially, it was described by Klein as an early developmental phase leading to the stabilizing of libidinal aggressive instincts. Later, Bion described it as a form of object relations leading towards the capacity for thought and symbolization in the context of adequate mothering. Rosenfeld defined projective identification as a primitive defence mechanism characteristic of severe personality disorders and as a mechanism present in psychotic states. Others have emphasized the interpersonal component, which is thought capable of evoking countertransference reactions in a therapeutic setting.

KLEINIAN PARADIGM

Based on Ferenczi's work on introjection–projection, Melanie Klein developed the concept of projective identification in her paper on schizoid mechanisms in 1946. Since then it has been widely used by analysts to describe a number of different clinical situations. As such its original meaning has become enlarged to contain a number of different concepts. More recently, Tansey and Burke have used the concept in relation to the notion of countertransference and empathy. In order to understand the possible relationship between these terms, I examine the historical origins of projective identification.

In Klein's initial formulation, projective identification was used to describe a primitive means of communication between mother and child. Described as a defence mechanism against anxiety, the good and bad aspects are projected out onto the caretaking figure, thereby making existence more tolerable. This corresponds to the notion of projection. The second phase refers to the identification of this split of affect in the other and a reintrojection of this vicarious experience. In this manner, the infant feels both persecuted and, at the same time, persecutory of the caretaking figure. There are difficulties with a literal rendition of Klein's theories but they have opened a way of understanding the early representational world of the infant and the structuring of early intra- and inter-psychic events.[59]

BIONION PARADIGM

Bion's formulation extended the notion of projective identification from an understanding of fantasy to the field of object-relations. By containing the feared and persecutory wishes and performing the functions of good-enough mothering, the mother allows the infant to experience relief and is thus reorientated to the reality of the immediate environment. It is the empathic apprehension by the mother of the infant's needs that leads to a diminution of discomfort and anxiety, and the subsequent capacity for undistorted object relations and thought.[60]

Conversely, in the absence of good-enough mothering Bion

---

[59] M. Klein, "Notes on Some Schizoid Mechanisms", in *Envy and Gratitude and Other Works, 1946-1963*, ed. Seymour Lawrence, New York: Delacorte Press, 1975.

[60] W.R. Bion, "Development of Schizophrenic Thought", *International Journal of Psychoanalysis*, **37**: 344-46, 1953; W.R. Bion, "Attacks on Linking", *International Journal of Psychoanalysis*, **40**: 308-15, 1959.

stated that anxiety is intensified, leading to further splitting, projection and fantasized retaliation by means of projective identification. The components of this process are also described alternately as being intra-psychic and interpersonal in that intra-psychic events develop to engage others. This may or may not invoke a corresponding valency within them. Thus for Bion, projective identification is a primitive developmental phenomenon that has implications for the emergent capacity for thinking and an undistorted experience of reality.

As stated earlier, this process is an important part of the communication between mother and child. It is by means of this process that the mother is able to carry the negative, intolerable affects of the child and help develop the child's ability for the capacity for tolerance of anxiety. Furthermore by linguistic meaning being attached to the unwanted affects, it helps to enlarge the symbolic capacity of the child. A clear understanding of the normal developmental nature of this process contributes to a clearer understanding of the distortions of development in the capacity to think, symbolize and develop individuality.

Furthermore, the concept of projective identification has implications for the development of the capacity for thought, creativity, aesthetic appreciation, empathy and symbolism, as expressed in a number of different ways by adults.

Bion considered the relationship of projective identification to thought and formulated an inverse relationship. In the presence of anxiety, thought may emerge in the form of symbolization in order to incorporate reality and thus lead to a modification of anxiety. If this anxiety is intolerable, it may result in a hypertrophied capacity for projective identification, thus subverting the capacity for symbolization and thought and lead to intensified projective identification.[61]

---

[61] W.R. Bion, "Attacks on Linking", *International Journal of Psychoanalysis*, **40**: 308-15, 1959; O.H.D. Blomfield, "Group Life →

I shall now discuss the views of some other writers concerning projective identification. Ogden views projective identification as a developmental and interpersonal phenomenon that may be manifested clinically, whereby projected fantasies evoke congruent feelings in others.[62] As such projective identification transcends the realm of the purely intrapsychic and becomes interpersonal as well. The feelings aroused in the recipient are incorporated as part of the phenomenon of projective identification, i.e. countertransference feelings parallel those of the projector. This differs from transference in that the therapist is seen, not only in a distorted way, but is also unconsciously pressured to experience the patient in a particular way. This countertransference response on the part of the therapist may develop into a concordant (i.e. identification with what the patient thinks of him or herself) or complementary identification (i.e. therapist's identification with what the patient thinks of the therapist), and thus reinforces the unconscious motivations of the patient.

Kernberg considers projective identification to be a lower-level defence mechanism that underlies severe character disorders along with other primitive defences, such as denial, primitive idealization, omnipotence and devaluation.[63] In distinction to the defence of projection, an affinity or empathy is thought to be maintained with the split-off part and may intentionally manifested as manipulative behaviour by the patient.

→ and Thinking", Circulated Paper to Training Group of the Aust. Group Psychotherapy Association.

[62] T.H. Ogden, "The Concept of Projective Identification", in M. Sandler (ed.), *Projection, Identification and Psychotherapeutic Technique*, New York: International Universities Press, 1987.

[63] O.F. Kernberg, "The Treatment of Patients with Borderline Personality Organization", *International Journal of Psychoanalysis*, **49**: 600-19, 1968.

Poder sees projective identification to be a repetition of a pathological childhood interaction between parent and child. However, there is a reversal of roles and the therapist is cast in the role of the bad child and treated in line with this perception.[64] More recently, Tyson and Spence see empathy as issuing from the therapist's successful internal processing of the patient's projective identification and thus establishing an attunement far deeper than is possible with verbal communication alone.[65]

Most of the articles on the subject emphasize the pathological aspects of projective identification, while the rest view the concept as confusing and not sufficiently articulated by existing psychoanalytic terms, such as projective counteridentification, and by forms of countertransference. However, by the enabling normative aspects of this process, projective identification could well be a basis for the development of empathy, mental representation, symbolization, creativity and imagination. Early primitive forms of relating and thought involving the mechanisms of projection, introjection and identification are also the basis of much that is healthy and adaptive, and the basis for communication and development of a personal language and meaning for the individual.

In relation to empathy, the notion of projective identification is used and described in similar ways. Both terms have a potentially intersubjective component and it is possible that both have a developmental component such that early functioning is a forerunner of later mature forms of functioning. Additionally,

---

[64] M.S. Poder, "Projective Identification: An Alternative Hypothesis", *Psychoanalytic Quarterly*, **56**: 431-51, 1987.

[65] R.L. Tyson, "Countertransference Evolution in Theory and practice", *Journal of the American Psychoanalytic Association*, **34**(2): 251-74, 1986.

both concepts are described as having defensive as well as adaptive roles, however, the defensive nature of projective identification is stressed within clinical work and healthy empathic functioning described as an asset.

It is possible that both functions fall along a gradient of functioning such that mature empathic function incorporates and transcends projective identification. As such, empathy could be described as a mature form of projective identification incorporating earlier forms of functioning. With mature function it would be possible to process projective identifications into a more mature self system capable of dealing with primitive psychic communication systems, however, the precise mechanisms of functioning remain uncertain.

POTENTIAL SPACE

In writing about the notion of potential space as a fundamental developmental concept, Winnicott introduced an important yet elusive concept.[66] As described by Ogden, potential space "refers to an intermediate area of experiencing that lies between fantasy and reality".[67] Specific forms of potential space by Winnicott include the play space, transitional object and phenomenon, the analytic space, the area of cultural experience and creative space.

In a detailed examination of the concept, Ogden explores the implications for the capacity to develop symbolization and subjectivity. The capacity for subjectivity is seen as being made possible, according to Ogden, by the developmental process

---

[66] D.W. Winnicott, "The Location of Cultural Experience", *International Journal of Psychoanalysis*, **48**: 368, 1967; D.W. Winnicott, "Transitional Objects and Transitional Phenomena", *International Journal of Psychoanalysis*, **34**: 89-97, 1953.

[67] T.H. Ogden, "On Potential Space", *International Journal of Psychoanalysis*, **66**: 129-41, 1985.

of differentiation from the sense of unity in the mother–child dyad. By utilizing Winnicott's notions of development, Ogden postulates a dialectic interaction between perceiver and perceived as the basis of subjectivity. Subjectivity is the basis for the development of awareness of self and other as objects of perception. Thus, the space of perception is occupied by symbols, the symbolized (object) and the reflexivity of the perceiver.

Initially, Ogden postulated that subjectivity is a potential in the mother–child unit. This initial holding environment is thought to be one where the needs of the infant are met by the condition of adequate mothering. With the onset of frustrations there is awareness of separateness and the existence of corporeal boundaries between mother and child. This awareness of aloneness in the presence of the mother is the heuristic emergence of subjectivity. This is elegantly described in a paper on "The Capacity to Be Alone", by Winnicott.[68] Thus, the capacity for symbolic function involves the interrelationship between three distinct entities — the symbol (thought), the symbolized (that which is being thought about) and the thinker (subjective self). The interactive emergent nature of this process allows for the capacity for awareness of a separate human being and thus the capacity for concern, mourning, empathy and creativity. In states of pathology, there is a differentiation between these three elements, leading to an excessive preoccupation with either reality or fantasy.

Ogden views empathy as a normal creative function of the potential space as distinct to projective identification. Empathy as a psychological process and form of object relating is seen to revolve around a dialectic of being and not being

---

[68] D.W. Winnicott, "The Capacity to Be Alone", *International Journal of Psychoanalysis*, **39:** 416-20, 1958.

another by means of trial identifications. This playful adoption of the identity of another is contrasted with the direct communication of projective identification where the therapist has little leeway to resist some form of identification. But the precise nature of this difference is not clearly articulated by the notion of subjectivity described by Winnicott. However, as described in the section above, the concept of subjectivity and space have important implications for an understanding of the means of accurate perception of the other. Perhaps it is by means of a series of playful trial identifications in this space that the reality of another is approached. The dialectic between self and other as objects mediated by the subjectivity of the perceiver, allows for the possibility of emergent meaning based on similarity and differences between self and other. The prototype for this process of emergent meaning between self and other is possibly the transition in the early mother–child relationship from a state of unity to a state of separateness, such that meaning arises out of difference and similarity.

REGRESSION

In describing the capacity of the observer to remain in touch with secondary process thinking and yet be able to derive information from primary processes, Northrup postulates an ability for regression without disruption of the mature ego to be an important concept towards an understanding of empathy. Likewise, others have considered this notion in relation to empathic function.

Schafer invokes the notion of "regression in the service of the ego", first defined by Kris as an important component of the empathic process. Kris introduced this idea to allow for a confluence between primary and secondary process thinking and it is similar to Hartman's use of the notion of "regressive adaptation", to Loewald's "regression in the service of the higher ego", and to Olnick's "regression in the service of the other".

Just as regression to primary process thinking can be seen to play a role in the therapeutic process, so, too, can empathy be seen as an incorporation of symbolic primary process to the more logical secondary processes of the therapist's thought. This combination of idiographic and meditative thought forms allows for the inclusion of memory, fantasy and imagination, as well as logico-deductive thinking, in arriving at a complex representational understanding of the other's reality. This inclusion of "non-scientific" subjective approaches to empathy meets with a number of responses in the literature which range from downright dangerous, to uncritical, and it being an essential component of empathy.[69]

INTROSPECTION

In the early twentieth century, psychology was considered the study of the contents of consciousness, particularly as defined by Wundt and Titchener. Titchener was also the first to translate empathy into English from the German root *Einfühlung*.[70]

However, with the rise of behaviourism, the emphasis shifted to the study of overt behaviour and the scientific status of introspection became suspect. Globus, in developing the research value of the introspective method, points out that although it falls into the domain of private areas of perception, it is amenable to training, measurement and development.[71] Exclusive use of the measurement of observable behaviours has lead to the exclusion of the equally complementary method of introspection.

---

[69] G.H. Northrup, *Psychoanalytic Issues in the Theory of Empathy* (Dissertation), Michigan: University Microfilms International, 1986 (Microfiche).

[70] E.B. Titchener, *Lectures on the Experimental Psychology of the Thought Processes*, New York: Macmillan, 1909.

[71] G.G. Globus, "Consciousness and the Brain", *Archives in General Psychiatry*, **29**(2): 167-77, 1973.

In formulating a concept of consciousness in relation to introspection and neural phenomena, Globus postulates a representational world at the interface of the phenomenal and processing (neural) worlds. This representational space that is proposed appears similar to that proposed by Ogden. The notion of a representational or potential space allows for the emergence into consciousness, meaning based on introspective or sensory qualia. Thus, Globus defines consciousness as that which refers

> specifically both to events which represent the world extrinsic to the nervous system as well as (to) events intrinsic to the nervous system which process representation events [*sic*].

The relevance of the understanding of representation to the process of empathy by means of introspection should now be apparent. Empathy may be based on phenomenal or sensory processing of the contents of experience. As such, the representation of the perceived other may be at a conscious or unconscious level. The introspective method may be a means of arriving at a clearer understanding of the latent and manifest contents of representation. Empirical studies on the relationship between the brain, introspection and empathy remain beset with problems of verifiability, yet there appears some preliminary evidence of correlation of activity. Furthermore, the definition of consciousness raises philosophical issues of different persuasions that make reductionistic definitions inoperable. However, the relationship of the introspective method to phenomenological method of exploring subjectivity will be discussed later.

Heinz Kohut, in proposing "vicarious introspection", appeared to be proposing a method of listening somewhat different from Freud's emphasis on "evenly hovering attention". In comparing and contrasting the two perspectives, Kainer suggests the fundamental difference to be including the significance of the real relationship alongside the transference analysis originally proposed by Freud. Kohut's stance of vicarious introspection is closer to the notion of participant observer proposed by Sullivan and is a fuller acknowledgement of the therapist's contributions to the patient's productions.[72] The internalization of the therapist as self-object possibly alters the therapeutic stance of the therapist from one of neutrality to participant observer, if only in the perception of the therapist and may lead to different formulations in the therapist's mind.

INTERIM SUMMARY

In comparing the notion of empathy with other psychoanalytic terms, a number of similarities and differences have emerged. Empathy plays an implicitly or explicitly avowed role in the therapeutic stance and in the understanding of the real and transferential aspects of the therapeutic relationship. The role of identification in relation to empathy was initially commented on by Fliess, and later by others, as a basis for arriving at some understanding of another by representing the other against some prior self-experience. This, however, leaves open the problem of whether we can truly empathize with another or whether we simply approach an understanding of another by reference to self. Perhaps an acknowledgement of difference based on a failure of trial identification with self leads to an empathic awareness of difference. Thus, the notion of identification seems an important mechanism for understanding the process of empathy.

Differentiating the notion of empathy from counter-transference appears difficult as both cover similar areas of

---

[72] R.G.K. Kainer, "From 'Evenly-Hovering Attention' to Vicarious Introspection: Issues of Listening in Freud and Kohut", *American Journal of Psychoanalysis*, **44**(1): 103-14, Spring 1984.

inquiry. Whereas countertransference is a specific clinical term, the applications of empathy extend to everyday existence. Furthermore, countertransference covers a wider range of responses by the therapist, in terms of both primitive and more sophisticated functioning of the ego. Thus, it appears wiser not to equate the two sorts of functions, although both involve the subjective appraisal of another. Countertransference appears to be a broader category of experience that may include empathic functioning. However, empathic functioning extends to everyday living and so is able to exist as a separate category of human existence.

The concepts of projection and introjection appear poorly defined in relation to empathy and, as discussed earlier, empathic functioning may incorporate mature forms of projective identification. Both projective identification and empathy appear to have an interpersonal as well as developmental nature and both may be experienced outside the therapeutic setting. However, the defensive aspects of projective identification appear to be discussed in relation to the therapeutic setting, in contrast to the adaptive aspects of empathic functioning.

The implications of potential space, regression and introspection are discussed in relation to the empathic process.

4

Implications for Further Clinical and Research Works

A. Redefinition of Empathy

A NOVEL approach was taken in examining the metatheoretical presuppositions inherent in clinical and theoretical accounts of empathy in the literature. The descriptive terms used in relation to the process often seemed ambiguous and to have acquired various meanings. Rather than provide further definitions, I have attempted to explicate existing clinical and theoretical definitions and to provide a general metatheoretical framework to examine ways in which this clinical process occurs.

The process of empathy is a clinical tool that provides the clinician with information about the subjective world of the patient. The clinical process as defined by the *Dorlands Medical Dictionary* was carried out traditionally at the bedside. However, in order to understand such a process a little better, I examine the metatheoretical principles by which it is conducted. From my research, a number of ways of conceptualizing empathy have emerged and these can only be offered tentatively, for future studies may lead to further developments in the field. Reflecting on Edith Stein's work on the problematic of empathy,[1] one is led to state that at

[1] Edith Stein, *On the Problem of Empathy*, tr. W. Stein, The Hague: Martinus Nijhoff, 1964.

best, models can only be explicated and that these will give way to better understanding is with future research.

Different, yet not mutually exclusive, ways of conceptualizing the process of empathy include an understanding of the cognitive, affective and perceptual processes involved. A cognitive understanding of the process of empathy has been given particular impetus with the works of Paiget, Kuhmerker and Hoffman (see the section on Cognitive Studies, p. 80). The complex range of processes leading to the conceptual understanding of another is based on the development of the necessary cognitive brain structures. Various analogues of the thinking process exist as for example, the logico-deductive models of reasoning and representation, or alternatively models of symbolic representation.

Rycroft views representation "as a general capacity of the mind which is based on perception and which may be used either by the primary or secondary process".[2] Representation of reality necessarily includes appraising the properties of the external object as well as the idiosyncratic prior patterns of representation of the perceiver. The *Oxford English Dictionary* defines representation as a process by which a description, portrayal, imagination, figure, place, likeness is called up before the mind or senses to serve as, or be meant of as a likeness.

In a comprehensive review entitled "Symbolism and Its Relationship to the Primary and Secondary Process",[3] Rycroft takes a wide view of the nature of symbolism and raises objections to restricting the concept to primary process functioning. Although he supports Klein's and Isaac's view that reality is subsumed by fantasy, Rycroft makes a further

---

2 Charles Rycroft, "Symbolism and Its Relationship to the Primary and Secondary Processes", *International Journal of Psychoanalysis*, **37**, 2-3, 1956.

3 Ibid.

distinction and defines imagination as "reality enhancing fantasies". Furthermore, words are also seen as symbols. Thus, an empathic attunement to language also provides information about the representational world of the patient.

My proposal is that the cognitive aspect involved in this process occurs by means of "double representation". Thus, a representation of self, be that in the form of memory, experience, part object, imagination, or linguistic trace, is juxtaposed with a collateral representation of the other. On the basis of congruence, deductions are made about similarities to oneself and, on the basis of non-congruence, an openness allows for difference. Similarities can be understood on the basis of analogues to common psychic phenomena, such as defined by the principles of psychoanalysis, and differences are acknowledged by an ontological openness to disclosure of oneself in the moment.

The metaphor of mental representation, utilizing symbols or symbolic construction, could be an underlying cognitive mechanism of empathy, whereby symbolic self representation is juxtaposed against a representation of another to arrive at an understanding of that other. Thus, the process of empathic perception and cognitive understanding remains in a state of change and may be modified by further perception, or in response to an empathetic communication to the patient. This representation of the other necessarily includes the appraisal of the properties of the external object as well as the idiosyncratic previous patterns of representation of the perceiver.

This cognitive aspect of empathic understanding seems to share some of the characteristics of participant observation as utilized, say, in the study of cultures different from that of the investigators. In order to understand a different cultural perspective, differences from and similarities to one's own culture are mapped. Thus, introspective and empirical phenomena are understood using the observer's own sign and symbol systems imaginatively. For a more meaningful understanding of another person, culture or event, and exploration of the conscious and unconscious processes, empathy can be a complementary tool.

CLINICAL STUDIES

In developing this perspective I would like to recount the following clinical incident in my own experience. I was called to a casualty of a teaching hospital in my capacity as a psychiatry registrar, to assess the case of a young, twenty-one-year-old engineering student, of Malaysian-Chinese background, who had taken an overdose of some twenty minor tranquillizers, following an agreed upon separation with his girlfriend. When introduced as the psychiatric registrar, the tall, thin and elegantly dressed youth, with some embarrassment, giggled. This seemed to me to be an inappropriate response, but on reflection I realized that in Malaysian culture, indeed, in much of Asian culture, psychiatry is viewed as being applicable only in the realm of asylums and such an encounter, therefore, would not be normal for ordinary citizens, who would be quite a bit embarrassed if they ever found themselves in the transcultural environ of psychiatry. Any suggestion that they might be in need of therapy would inevitably provoke the response that this must be a comic situation and so can be laughed off to stave the pain of having to take the situation as projected by others near him.

In allowing my memory to retrieve my experience of the perception of distinct place and assessment of psychiatry in Asian culture, it was possible to understand the significance of the giggle: a metonymic device of deferral (in cultural-social terms as well as to appraise the source of the obvious embarrassment) a metaphor for displacement on the part of the patient. Thus, in allowing for a juxtaposition of my own experience of an aspect of Asian cultural perception of psychiatry, I was able to recall information relevant to the particular (and peculiar) situation and to understand intuitively and cognitively, rather than rationally and judgementally, a distinctive inner-world experience of another. Thus, an initial "double representation" allowed me to access my own understanding of cultural differences in the perception of psychiatry. However, the representation also allowed for a representation of difference in my own case in respect of gender, culture, education, status and so on, and so allowed for an exploration of the motivation behind the patient taking the overdose. Thus, this instance of mental representation allowed me to empathetically appraise, understand and explicate the immediate predicament of another.

In the understanding of affective states, psychoanalytic theory has done much to elucidate various responses of the psychiatrist and patient. These responses were reviewed in the section on "Empathy in Relationship to Other Psychotherapeutic Categories" (Chapter 3b). The process of identification, projection, projective identification and countertransference shed light on the relative contribution of these processes towards an understanding of the communication of affect. Affect is defined as feeling, emotion and desire in the *Oxford English Dictionary*. The direct transmission of affect as studied by Tomkins and expanded on by Basch is postulated by them to be the basis for affect development and also development of affect attunement with another person. The development of moral development and reasoning involves more complicated cognitive processes, as well as an understanding of the affective process of empathy.

To understand affect transmission and empathy, the notion of projective identification was explored so as to provide metaphors for this mode of understanding, which seems to bypass complex cognitive reasoning. The analogy of empathy as a process akin to mature projective identification is a model of the affective aspect of empathy that I wish to propose.

Just as in common parlance empathic understanding may be characterized as a sort of "gut feeling", as an intuitive understanding of a complex process without resorting to an elaborate set of rational logical premises or behavioural indices. Rather than regurgitate the literature on projective identification, I would like to propose empathy as being akin to the process of mature projective identification where the received perception is not reduced haphazardly, but held, processed, used as a source of information about the affective state of the patient, and perhaps examined and appraised by means of secondary cognitive empathic processes before an interpretation is made or not made, as the case may be.

CLINICAL EXAMPLES

I would like now to illustrate the foregoing discussion with examples drawn from my own clinical experience.

Example 1

When asked to review a thirty-five-year-old Italian woman who had frequent admissions for catatonic schizophrenia, I was overcome with a sense of forlornness as I observed the patient's distressed disposition, seated as she was in a ward, clad in a hospital gown, in a posture of paralysis. I was prompted to say to the patient that we would speak only when it was safe enough for her to so do. The patient, over a period of three days, began to eat, drink and, at my very next visit, she stood up and spoke, saying, "I know you, you are Dr Sharma". It seemed that some of her affect of despair had been transmitted to me and that I had, without engaging in logical reasoning, responded with my "gut feeling" in the form of an intervention.

Example 2

While working therapeutically with a very dependent female cello teacher, I found that it was my attention and "being with" which seemed vital to the process. Over the weeks, I found that as soon as my attention waned or wandered, she would immediately question me as to whether I had heard her at all. On one occasion, in a session with the patient, after a very long and tiring day, I was conscious of struggling to maintain an uninterrupted attention to what was being said. But she remained unusually quiet throughout the session. However, after midnight that same day she called me on the telephone to say that she was having a panic attack and was wondering if I or anyone else would really understand her. This was unusual as the patient had never before called me that late and never has since. In a subsequent session, the patient talked for the first time of her cold and undemonstrative mother whom she had never felt understood by.

On reflection, I realized that the patient was attuned to my varying capacity for empathic affect in-tuneness. Thus, my empathic failure led the patient to talk about her "absent mother" who had been emotionally unavailable, largely due to medical illness and had in fact, died at the early age of forty. In retrospect, it was my affective availability and subsequent lapse in empathy that led to a further exploration of the phenomenon.

In the above instances, it was empathic attunement similar to a "gut feeling" understanding, that led, in the first case, to the appropriate intervention and, in the second case, to an explication of early deprivation of maternal empathic attunement. Thus, holding some unwanted affect until such time that the patient is able to work with that affect seems to be a process that may be useful in working with the more seriously disturbed patient. Such a practice, however, presupposes that the therapist's self-system is able to perceive the process instead of returning the affect inappropriately. Thus, in assimilating the affect-introject, the disturbing affect is metaphorically held until such time as it can be brought to the understanding of the patient.

In arriving at an understanding of this process a "double affective representation" may occur where a vicarious experience of the other is matched with an early primitive pre-verbal affective experience, be that of jealousy, pain, joy, or despair, to arrive at an understanding of the experience of the other. If this process of attunement is understood, then an empathic holding or interpretation may result in communicating to the patient either verbally or pre-verbally the experience of being understood.

A third model which overlaps with the previous model is that of empathy being akin to a transitional space, which subsumes both cognitive and affective processes, such that a process of suspension of cognitive logical reasoning or affective state occurs in order to prevent a premature understanding of the other. Hence, empathic perception may allow for the emergence of fantasy intermingled with reality; fantasy that has hitherto remained hidden in the subconscious of the other. Drawing on Winnicott's work on children and his notion of transitional space, I refer back to the discussion in the previous section on empathy in relation to transitional or potential space.

Example 3

In my first year as a psychiatric trainee, I held the position of registrar for a period of six months in a forensic establishment. My tasks were related to crisis intervention and, by and large, the daily administration and management of ward and outpatient. In the rather antiquated environment, there was little in the way of a therapeutic ward milieu: patients were managed generally by medication and there were few therapeutic activities.

Shortly after beginning the placement, my attention was drawn to the childlike face of a patient who stood for long hours looking into the staffroom as a I sat and completed my notes during the early and late hours of the day. On inquiry, I discovered that the patient suffered from schizophrenia and had been in institutional care almost since birth. He had also lived in boys' homes, and in prison, before being committed to the psychiatric forensic unit. Later, the patient would follow me around the ward as I attended to the various medical duties. As I came to know him better, he would often talk about his fantasy of a being a writer or an Oxford don and so forth. On numerous occasions he wrote off to different universities, requesting encyclopaedia, books, tutorials, etc.

Having noted his behaviour, I led a discussion for five minutes every ward meeting on the subject of the patient. It gradually emerged that staff were able to provide the patient with a typewriter, a desk, a briefcase. They then set him up with his writing gear in a corner which he began to regard as his office.

At the instigation of the nursing staff, he was provided with addresses of Amnesty International and other organizations. Within a short time the patient started to write and send letters to various parts of the world. During this period, he successfully requested a community visitor and began to be visited regularly by an elderly retired chiropractor, who was able to take him shopping and allow him to choose clothes for himself. The provision of a non-judgemental space within the staff ward rounds led to considerable developmental progress. In creating a reflective space about the patient's needs, possibilities emerged, often without a specific intervening cognitive or affective process, rather a sort of space where different things began to emerge from, and which subsumed both affective and cognitive processes.[4]

[4] S.L. Olinick, "A Critique of Empathy and Sympathy", in *Empathy I* (ed. Lichtenberg J. et al.), pp. 137-66.

In this example, empathy could be conceptualized as an ongoing experience that includes the capacity for cognitive appraisal, mature projective identification, mental representations and symbolism. The locus of this function could be contained in a transitional emergent space wherein sensory data are collated with introspective memory, desires and imagination.

This fluid model of empathy would need to be seen as an independent mental act and, although based on primitive defence mechanisms and existing cognitive structures, it also derives much from other non-pathological forms of experience, such as the capacity for symbolism and language.

In attempting to elucidate the process of empathy, I have emphasized the cognitive, affective and transitive nature of the processes involved. To define the process further, means of study more appropriate to subjective states would need to be sought. Further clinical and research directions could arise from close studies of the mother–child affective relationship as a metaphor for a process of empathy; sophisticated multidimensional psychological studies are already providing an understanding of the cognitive and behavioural processes of empathy. In addition, studies on moral development and reasoning hold promise for a better understanding of these processes in relation to empathy. Lastly, the phenomenological method may be a more appropriate mode of exploring subjective states. These themes are explored in later chapters.

B. Further Research And Clinical Models

Having stated the difficulties in the definition of empathy, the difficulties in defining development of empathy are even more complex. Developmental perspectives have emerged from the areas of social-cognitive psychology, infant studies and psychoanalysis.

DEVELOPMENTAL STUDIES

Social Cognitive Studies

The work of Kolhberg, Dewey and Paiget are seen as both milestones towards conceptualizing cognitive development as phase specific and continuous.[5] Conceptualization of intellectual and moral development as a series of sequential and irreversible stages provides a model for studying the development of empathy. Such models have been proposed by a number of writers, for example, Feinbach, O'Keefe, Hoffman in Goldstein and Michaels.[6] However, such theories have been slow to emerge and may reflect the difficulties in operationalizing the term. Furthermore, Kuhmerker suggests that the notion of a priori existence of empathy at birth may have hindered the earlier emergence of a developmental notion.[7]

Developmental models presented in the literature have placed different degrees of emphasis on affective, cognitive, social, perceptual and communicative aspects of development. Feinbach and Hoffman's models, although being multi-dimensional, place emphasis on the vicarious affective experience in contradistinction to social cognition and role taking. By contrast, in Keefe's model, cognitive comprehension is central to the empathic experience. Here the cognitive model

---

[5] L. Kuhmerker, "Learning to Care: The Development of Empathy", *J. Moral Education*, **5**(1): 25-33, 1975; L. Kuhmerker, "Social Interaction and the Development of a Sense of Right and Wrong in Young Ren", *J. Moral Education*, **5**(3): 257-64, 1976; D. Silver, "Introductory Remarks: Developmental Aspects of Empathy", in Lichtenberg et al. (eds.), *Empathy II*, 1985, pp. 3-8.

[6] A.P. Goldstein and Y.G Michaels, *Empathy, Development, Training and Consequences*, Hillsdale, NJ: Lawrence Erlbaum, 1985.

[7] L. Kuhmerker, "Social Interaction and the Development of a Sense of Right and Wrong in Young Ren", *J. Moral Education*, **5**(3): 257-64, 1976.

is seen as going beyond stimulus perception, affective identification and role appropriateness towards complex judgements, moral conceptions and actions. The findings from these studies remain tentative and it is uncertain whether affective empathy precedes cognitive processing and the nature of the ongoing interaction between affect and cognition.

Maternal–Infant Studies: Relational, Maternal and Infant Aspects of the Development of Empathy

Relational aspects: Infant observation studies show the interrelatedness of the empathic capacities of mother and child. The development of an empathic capacity is dependent on the empathic abilities of the mother, which in turn reflect the mother's personality and upbringing. The mother is the first other of contact, as such she provides the first model of caring and sharing as well as her own cultural-shaping influences. This is perceived differently by the growing infant at different stages, due to the ongoing maturational, physical, affective, cognitive and neuronal components of the infant's world. The interaction between mother and infant can best be understood as a synergy of development and relatedness for both mother and child. Although this is readily evident in relation to the child, it is less visibly so in relation to the mother. Nevertheless, it is a time of profound change for mothers who are required to negotiate physical, psychological and often other lifestyle changes, perceived through a personality more mature than the child's but which is changing. Birth is a developmental milestone for both mother and child and the way this is experienced will revolve around the mother's previous developmental experiences, personality, defences and coping mechanisms.

Having placed this discussion within the confines of the complexity of the emergent developmental–relational field, where the speed and fluidity of interchange are difficult to quantify, there are certain common elements of this dialogue that can be seen across social and cultural boundaries. Genetic unfolding is the bond between the two key players in the field, which under normal circumstances, leads to the development of meaningful communication. The development of this matrix is not only essential for the survival of the infant, but is also the necessary environment through which the trajectories of development are launched. The inner world of the mother is powerfully accessed by the neonate, leading to the development of a complex relational field.

Silver, in using a metaphor from the science fiction movie Extra-Terrestrial (ET) 1982, underscores the movement from affective resonance to shared language.[8] It is the private world and language of the mother that shapes and responds to the affective and physical needs of the infant that, in turn, leads to representational thinking, empathic capacity for self (or self-empathy), and much later, for others. This relational model has implications for a further understanding of the intersubjective component of empathy.

MATERNAL ASPECTS

It is obvious that the mother's responses will vary in complexity from basic physical responses, to more complex perceptual–emotional responses to an experience of shared joy and play. Lipton and Tonge present a description of mothering behaviour that, although constant in form, may vary in style.[9] This behaviour involves a state of initial togetherness, holding and mutuality. The second function is of pushing out and encouraging separateness, leading to a comfortable separateness under optimal circumstances and the third function is to reunite or return to the mother's protection.

---

[8] D. Silver, "Introductory Remarks: Developmental Aspects of Empathy", in Lichtenberg et al. (eds.), *Empathy II*, 1985, pp. 3-8.

[9] G. Lipton and B. Tonge, "The Essence of Mothering Children Under Five", in *Modern Perspective in the Psychiatry of Infancy*, ed. J.G. Howells, New York: Brunner/Mazel, 1979, pp. 191-21.

The timing of this will depend on the mother's empathic awareness of the child's inner needs. It is difficult to operationalize further this intuitive empathic state of mothering wherein account is taken of the internal worlds of mother and child as well as the external reality: "empathic mothering is the psychic correlate of what is observed in successful mothering behaviour". This intuitive empathic state is in contrast to psychoanalytic models that concentrate on specific aspects of mothering, such as breastfeeding, which are difficult to quantify. Others have developed observational scales of mothering from which inferences are drawn about the capacity for relatedness by the mother.

Winnicott, in describing primary maternal preoccupation, draws attention to the heightened sensitivity akin to illness behaviour displayed by mothers prior to and shortly after birth.[10] Broussard, in a longitudinal study, postulates that maternal empathy is a correlation of maternal self-esteem and that this in turn correlates to the development of a positive self-image and capacity for empathy in children.[11] Burlingham takes this further to suggest that the conscious and unconscious conflicts of the mother are powerful influences on the child's developing capacities for empathy.[12] By the process of observation, the child arrives at inferences about the world of the mother that, in turn, shape the representational world of the infant and eventually the capacity for mature independence with the capacity for relatedness and intimacy.

---

[10] D.W. Winnicott, "The Theory of the Parent-Infant Relationship", in D.W. Winnicott ed. *The Maturational Process and the Facilitating Environment*, New York: International Universities Press, 1965.

[11] E.R. Broussard, "Maternal Empathy: Its Relation to Emerging Self Representations and Empathy in Infants", in *Empathy II* (ed. Lichtenberg, J. et al.), pp. 81-106.

[12] D. Burlingham, "Empathy Between Infant and Mother", *Journal American Psychoanalitic Association*, **15**(4): 764-80, 1964.

INFANT ASPECTS

To recapitulate briefly, infant studies have focused on the contributory factors coming from the child, on contributions of the mother and on the field of empathic interplay and mutual responsivity. Studies of the infant's contributions have investigated a wide range of areas such as temperament, perception, sharing of motor responses, i.e. motor synchrony, nature of affective resonance, and the cognitive and psychic developments necessary for the process of empathy to emerge.

Recent studies suggest the ability of very young infants to discern and, in turn, imitate facial expressions. The relation between affect perception and experience remains at the level of conjecture but ties in with the hypothesis that motor mimicry is a means of empathic understanding. This hypothesis relates to the theory of emotion proposed by Darwin and James wherein the subjective experience of emotion was thought to be caused by the perception of physiological changes, which, in turn, are thought to be the basis of the emotions. This is echoed by the more recent work of Tomkins, studying the autonomic basis of emotional states. Tomkins postulates nine basic emotional states, which are brought about by distinct patterns of autonomic reactivity. These studies relate to the perception of emotion that precedes the development of social perception, moral development and altruism. Such a model of empathic development has much in common with Lipp's theory of empathy, i.e. empathic perception by means of motor mimicry and projection. Condon's analysis of a series of picture frames of mother–infant interaction provides an interesting insight into the communication of form.[13] The mother's body, tone and voice modulations convey a subtle and precise message to the perceptual world of the infant, i.e in a way

---

[13] W.S. Condon, "Communication and Empathy", in *Empathy II*, 1984, pp. 34-58.

similar to primary maternal preoccupation, attuned to the nuances of the evolution of this shared language.

Demos sees empathy as the essential element in the therapeutic and developmental process and affective resonance as the basis of the development of a shared language.[14] Drawing on the writings of Tomkins, he describes as a biologically innate response. Demos describes six types of exchanges based on observational data, which can result in a number of different outcomes.

Bergman and Wilson, drawing on psychoanalytic literature, especially Mahler's developmental framework and Piagetian cognitive notions, postulate a phase-specific development of empathy.[15] They suggest that empathy develops at eighteen months of age when the capacity for representational thinking and symbolic fantasy emerge. This coincides with the development of cognitive maturity towards the ability to comprehend physical and psychic separateness. Prior to this phase, apprehensions of the other were thought to be by way of selective cues and the scripting of the unconscious to occur by a series of images. It is with the acquisition of language that complex layers of representations of self and other emerge. It is postulated that it is with the emergence of this capacity for representation that self–other boundaries emerge and, so correctly speaking, also the capacity for concern for the other. Prior to this time, self–other differences were thought not to exist.

In considering the contributions from psychoanalytic and infant studies, Stern places imitation and affect relatedness at

---

[14] V. Demos, "Empathy and Affect: Reflections on Infant Experience", in *Empathy II*, 1984, pp. 9-34.

[15] A. Bergman and A. Wilson, "Thoughts About Stages on the Way to Empathy and the Capacity for Concern", in *Empathy II*, 1984, pp. 59-80.

two ends of a spectrum.[16] Mere motor mimicry replicates the form of communication whereas affect attunement allows for resonance of feeling. Mirroring, inter-subjectivity and empathy are seen as poorly defined components of the relational field. Stern's developmental model comes close to the multi-dimensional models proposed by Hoffman and Feshbach who propose an additional social-cognitive phase to imitation and affect attunement.[17]

Psychoanalytic Formulations

Psychoanalytic formulations on the development of empathy place emphasis on different structural aspects of intrapsychic development. Loewald, Winnicott and Spitz pay attention to the affect attunement between mother and child as evident in the processes of mutual mirroring. Others have placed the origins in the symbiotic phase while others place the origins after self–object differentiation which appears between fourteen to eighteen months. However, no comprehensive accounts include the notion of empathy developing as a separate trajectory.

COGNITIVE STUDIES

Goldstein and Michaels[18] evaluate the cognitive research studies performed on the subject of empathy. A number of distinct stages of study begin to emerge retrospectively. Prior to 1960, beginning with the person perception studies of Darwin, investigators became interested in the elucidation of

---

[16] D. Stern, *The Interpersonal World of the Infant: A View from Psychoanalysis and Developmental Psychology*, New York: Basic Books, 1985.

[17] A.P. Goldstein and Y.G Michaels, *Empathy, Development, Training and Consequences*, Hillsdale, NJ: Lawrence Erlbaum, 1985.

[18] Ibid.

a general ability for sensitive and accurate perception of others. In a comprehensive review, Kuhmerker[19] concluded that empathy remained difficult to operationalize and measure. In the last two decades, person perception studies have declined with a corresponding rise in humanistic (client-centred), social psychological and developmental psychology studies. During this time, psycho-analytical studies have proliferated, however, each study has disregarded the research undertaken outside its domain of interest. More recently, as in the work of Goldstein and Michaels, there is a move towards incorporating research findings from divergent areas into multidimensional models.

Early person–perception studies by Cronbach, Kohler and Gordon were designed to assess physical postures as representing mental states. However, person perception was not differentiated from object perception and, as such the measurement of affect, effect of situational variables and relationship of perceiver to perceived was precluded by the design of the experiments.

The client-centred approach to therapy pioneered by Maslow and Rogers engendered an analysis of the therapist's empathic/affective stance in relation to the process and outcome of psychotherapy. Initially, studies substantiated the finding that the therapist's empathic qualities were associated with successful outcome.[20] Later studies have queried the construct validity of these findings, since a positive outcome is correlated with other aspects of the therapist's personality and the therapeutic situation, and standard methods of assessment have long been criticized as lacking constructive validity.

---

[19] L. Kuhmerker, "Learning to Care: The Development of Empathy", *J. Moral Education*, **5**(1): 25-33, 1975.

[20] C.B. Truax and K.M. Mitchell, "Research on Certain Therapist Interpersonal Skills in Relation to Process and Outcome", in A.E. Bergin and S.L. Garfield (eds.) *Handbook of Psychotherapy and Behavior Change: An Empirical Analysis*, New York: Wiley, 1971.

Cognitive developmental studies have been slow to emerge in the field. Kuhmerker sees this as the result of difficulties in conceptualizing the concept clearly, as well as the notion of empathy existing a priori instead of developing in a phase-specific, stepwise manner. The works of Kohlberg, Dewey and Piaget are seen as milestones towards the conceptualization of intellectual, moral and, by analogy, empathic development as a series of sequential and irreversible stages. Complex developmental models encompassing perceptual, motor, affective and social-cognitive features are proposed by a number of researchers.[21] With George Herbert Mead's work the situational context of empathy as distinct from the search for a persistent trait, came to the forefront. Role-playing was seen as a means of developing interpersonal images that enhance the ability to understand the possible range of behaviours exhibited by another person in a given situation. A comprehensive review of the studies outlining this perspective is offered by Deutsch and Madle.[22]

Despite the range of conceptualizations of empathy offered, few empirical advances have been made. This could be a reflection of the lack of operational definitions of empathy and the difficulty in applying empirical research methods to non-quantifiable phenomena involving a complex interplay of factors, such as affect and cognition. Jacobs and Williams[23] in criticizing the "scienticism" inherent in empathy research,

---

[21] A.P. Goldstein and Y.G Michaels, *Empathy, Development, Training and Consequences*, Hillsdale, NJ: Lawrence Erlbaum, 1985.

[22] F. Deutsch and R.A. Madle, "Empathy: Historic and Current Conceptualizations, Measurement and a Cognitive Theoretical perspective human development", *Human Development*, **18**(4): 267-87, 1975.

[23] D. Jacobs, and V. Williams, "Clinical Theory and Scientism: Empathy Research as a Case Study", *Journal of Humanistic Psychology*, **23**(1): 79-96, 1983.

suggest that clinical theory resists meaningful investigation by such quantitative methods aimed at the formalization of concepts rather than at an extrication of meaning.

It is beyond the scope of this inquiry to address the critiques of the foundationalist epistemology of science, except to state that these critiques are relevant to the emergence of non-empiricist methods of study of human subjectivity. The metapsychology of psychoanalysis, while providing valuable insights into the realm of the unconscious, has, until recently, excessively reified the domains of the unconscious and the conscious. In a critical account of Freud's theory of reality, Casey raises issues related to the split between reality and fantasy: reality being seen as an a priori given as distinct from the notion of experiential reality, such as Husserl's "life-world" and Heidegger's "bewzg-in-the-world".

Later developments in the area of object–relations and self–object relations have attempted to account for the reciprocal relations between self and object reality and self and other's reality. Numerous critiques from within the domain of psychoanalysis address these issues, which, again, go beyond the scope of this work.

The dichotomy between external and internal leaves little space to allow for a notion of emergent subjective experience that transcends both poles. In reviewing the literature on psychoanalysis and empathy, it became apparent to me that a solipsistic point of view either introspectionistic or extrospective leads to an incomplete conceptualization of the process of perception of the other and a cognizance of one's own inner reality. The study of observable behaviour, or of fantasy alone, precludes a full examination of the phenomenon of empathy.

The validity of various forms of investigation can only be decided on criteria of internal consistency and parsimony. The methods of natural science allow for the study of observable behaviour just as the study of psychoanalysis allows for the understanding of unconscious motivations. The application of phenomenology and hermeneutics to an understanding of concepts such as empathy at best raises further questions about the meaning and understanding of another's existence.

In the section that follows I shall briefly review the phenomenological method and propose a phenomenological research paradigm for the further study of empathy based on the work of Amadeo Giorgi. In outlining a possible alternative strategy towards studying empathy, I do not attempt to offer an analysis of the phenomenological method or its relationship to hermeneutics and the domain of intersubjectivity.

PHENOMENOLOGICAL METHOD

The phenomenological method, for the study of psychological phenomena, as adapted for example by Giorgi, seems to offer a means for further uncover the meaning of empathy.[24] The aim of such a method is to arrive at unconcealing the essential features of a phenomenon, i.e. the object of experience, by eliminating influences and encumbrances from extraneous factors.

For Husserl, phenomenology was concerned with the study of pure phenomenon: the *logos* of the *phenomena*, which was captured in his motto "back to the fact itself", meaning "a return to the essentially given in the structure of experience". To pursue this logical (as distinct from empirical and ontological) investigation, Husserl advocated that one had to

---

[24] A. Giorgi, "Theoretical Justification for the Use of Descriptions in Psychological Research", in P.D. Ashworth, A. Giorgi and A.J.J. Koning (eds.), *Qualitative Research in Psychology: Proceedings of the International Association for Qualitative Research*, Pittsburgh, PA: Dusquesne University Press, 1986; A. Giorgi, *Phenomenology and Psychological Research*, Pittsburgh, PA: Dusquesne University Press, 1985.

put aside, or "bracket", thought and all perceptual and ontological presuppositions in order to let the pure "essence" of the phenomenon under examination emerge. This process is known as "phenomenological reduction" or *epoché*, and it is much discussed in contemporary philosophy.[25]

Intentionality is a key concept in phenomenology. Franz Brentano initially described intentionality as representations within consciousness. Brentano's view was that the mental is characterized by a peculiar directedness towards an object or by intentionality. Husserl went a step further in maintaining that in all such directness there is a content of the mental that is unique to each experience.[26] This content (*noema*) represents the "meaning" or semantic structure of the experience, and it characterizes the mode in which the object is given (or inexistent) in consciousness. This intrinsic mental phenomenon is what phenomenology attempts to discern and describe in the intentional state. It is important, as J.N. Mohanty notes, from the Husserlian perspective to stress that the content, or *noema*, is the *meaning* and not some picture or imagistic representation of the object; it is not a substitute for the object.[27] The content presents rather a *noesis* to how the object is being experienced and *interpreted* (i.e. its semantic structure). The emergence of meaning, then, leads to the discovery of essence. The mental act in which this occurs is called the intentional act; a network of intentional acts form a self-enclosed mental life through whose internal *contents* and their collectivity the world of the individual derives its constitutive meanings or senses.

---

25 Edmund Husserl, *The Idea of Phenomenology* (tr. W.P. Alston and G. Nakhnika), The Hague: Martinus Nijhoff, 1964.

26 Edmund Husserl, *Ideas* (tr. W.R. Boyce Gibson), London: Allen and Unwin, 1958.

27 J.N. Mohanty, "Levels of Understanding Intentionality", *The Monist*, **69**(4): 505-20; October, 1986; see also *Phenomenology and Ontology*, The Hague: Martinus Nijhoff, 1970.

More than simply directedness towards an object, intentionality here indicates the internal process and way by which the world is experienced, related to and interpreted by the individual.[28] Without understanding the inner mechanism of the meaning-conferring act of conscious experience, i.e. its intentionality, a clinician or therapist would be left with reporting outward behaviour, impressionistic cues and inferences about the *inner life-world* of the client or patient.

Thus, by concentrating on experience, devoid of assumptions, and by utilizing imagination, meaning and essences are arrived at.[29] Such a method is thought to be a systematic means of gathering knowledge about objects of one's experience. This introduction is only a brief account of the comprehensive work stemming from Husserl. Later developments include the works of Sartre,[30] Heidegger and Gadamer, who maintained the interest in the search for an existentialist interpretive meaning (hermeneutics) of being-in-the-world (*Daseiri*) and the unavoidable limitations (historical and egological) of all conscious experience. Thus, they broadened the arena of investigation beyond the immediate objects of experience, such as to matrices of tradition as encoded in texts. This intentional sense may not

---

[28] J.N. Mohanty, *The Concept of Intentionality*, Warren Green: St Louis, revised as *Husserl's Concept of Intentionality* (Analecta Husserliana), vol. ID, Dordrecht: Reidel & Co., 1972, see also Edmund Husserl's *Theory of Meaning*, The Hague: Martinus Hijhoff, 1964; J.N. Mohanty, "Levels of Understanding Intentionality", *The Monist*, **69**(4): 505-20; October, 1986; see also *Phenomenology and Ontology*, The Hague: Martinus Nijhoff, 1970.

[29] Edward S. Casey, *Imaging: A Phenomenological Study*, Bloomington: Indiana University Press, 1979.

[30] Jean-Paul Sartre, "Intentionality: A Fundamental Feature of Husserl's Phenomenology" (tr. J. Fell), *Journal of the British Society for Phenomenology*, **I**: 4-5, 1970.

be private simply to the individual but may be a socially shareable characteristic of people at a particular given time. Hence Freud, who had earlier associations with Husserl, was able to speak of the "puritanical" intentionality of the Victorian era or of Vienna around the turn of the century. Herbert Spiegelberg (died 1990) gives a comprehensive account of the relevant key figures in this tradition of phenomenological-hermeneutics.[31]

The work of Amadeo Giorgi has led to a revival of interest in the implications of phenomenology for psychology. As the methods of empirical science have come under increasing attack, it is little wonder that this timely revival is thought to provide scope for the explication of human phenomena, both normal and pathological. In developing Husserl's notion of phenomenological reduction as a means of studying human behaviour, Giorgi continues in the tradition of Binswanger, Jaspers, Merleau-Ponty[32] and other early psychologists inspired by phenomenology.

A relevant critique of this method is put forward by the phenomenologist J.N. Mohanty.[33] Such a method appears well

---

[31] Herbert Spiegelberg, *Phenomenology in Psychology and Psychiatry: A Historical Introduction*, Evanston: Northwestern University Press, 1972.

[32] M. Merleau-Ponty, M. Merleau-Ponty, "The Child's Relations with Others", in *The Sociology of Childhood: Essential Readings*, ed. Jenks C. Batsford, Academic and Educational 1982; M. Merleau-Ponty, *The Phenomenology of Perception* (tr. Colin Smith), London: Routledge, Kegan & Paul, 1962.

[33] J.N. Mohanty, *The Concept of Intentionality*, Warren Green: St Louis, revised as *Husserl's Concept of Intentionality* (Analecta Husserliana), vol. ID, Dordrecht: Reidel & Co., 1972, see also Edmund Husserl's *Theory of Meaning*, The Hague: Martinus Hijhoff, 1964; J.N. Mohanty, "Levels of Understanding Intentionality", *The Monist*, **69**(4): 505-20; October, 1986; see also *Phenomenology and Ontology*, The Hague: Martinus Nijhoff, 1970.

suited to elucidating the distinctive content or *noema* constitutive of the structure of empathy. The intersubjective relational nature of empathy takes into account that the human person is neither subject nor object but a relational space. Therefore, the method captures a description of the lived and situated empathy, not the subjective or objective experience but the interrelational space.

A comprehensive account of the method, as initially articulated by Giorgi, is available in his writings. The aim of the method is to discover the structures of experience in a rigorous and systematic way. The method involves four stages. In the first stage, a verbal "naïve", non-reflective report of a phenomenon experienced by a subject is collected by the researcher. In the second stage, the "naïve" description is examined and an initial reduction carried out.

This initial reduction leads to the emergence of "meaning units" relevant for a psychological understanding of the particular experience being studied. A number of possible meaning units could be derived from this stage. In the third stage, essential themes are identified from an analysis of the meaning units. This stage leads to the merging of an insight into the fundamental meaning of the experience. The contextual nature of the experience places the phenomenon in the lived world. Thus, a thorough examination of the objects of experience necessarily locates this recorded experience in an awareness of the location of this experience into a larger contextual frame of meaning.

A further feature of this method builds on the intentionality of consciousness. The relational aspect of human nature situates the study of human beings within an intersubjective field, which is its specific context. While the location of intentionality was initially developed and located within conscious experience, Georgi argues that the location of intentionality can also be applicable to the preconscious realm, and even extended to the larger area of subjective experience.[34]

It is beyond the purview of this study to review the expanding field of phenomenological psychology to include an understanding of the norms of everyday living as well as the domain of psychopathology, which is better provided by Fischer.[35] However, I would propose that this method of research may apply to a study of empathy, which is an attempt to return to the description of the lived experience, a subsequent reduction to arrive at the essential nature of the phenomena and the relevance of this to the immediately lived world as well as for therapeutic intervention. It is possible that the use of the phenomenological method will help find new ways of understanding the meaning of empathy.

---

[34] A. Giorgi, "Theoretical Justification for the Use of Descriptions in Psychological Research", in P.D. Ashworth, A. Giorgi and A.J.J. Koning (eds.), *Qualitative Research in Psychology: Proceedings of the International Association for Qualitative Research*, Pittsburgh, PA: Dusquesne University Press, 1986; J.N. Mohanty, "Levels of Understanding Intentionality", *The Monist*, **69**(4): 505-20; October, 1986; see also *Phenomenology and Ontology*, The Hague: Martinus Nijhoff, 1970.

[35] W.J. Fischer, "On the Phenomenological Approach to Psychology", *Journal of Phenomenological Psychology*, **17**: 65-76, Spring, 1986.

5

Discussion and Conclusion

In order to understand the clinical phenomenon of empathy, an extensive literature search was conducted. At the completion of that search, it was still formidably difficult to formulate a definition of this clinical concept.

However, a number of perspectives emerged that raised a number of questions about the nature of empathy. Historically, the term came from and was popularized by usage within the field of aesthetics. Its usage was then extended to the fields of religion, anthropology, comparative and cross-cultural studies, and philosophy. Within psychoanalysis, the term was used in relation to psychoanalytic technique, but over the past thirty years, it has been used by the proponents of Self Psychology.

Examining the relevant writings on empathy reveals a plethora of perspectives, often contradictory and confusing. A closer examination reveals interchangeable uses of the term as well as difficulties in defining exactly the process of empathic appraisal of another. I would suggest that these difficulties in defining and using the term are inherent and are accentuated by tensions relating to fundamental differences concerning the language and politics of psychoanalysis.

Specific issues raised in the study of empathy are:

a. the problem of accurately perceiving another;

b. whether the experiences of another can be

comprehended on the basis of purely intra-psychic theories as distinct to the relational and interpersonal elements;

c. whether empathy is a free-standing a priori category of experience, or is a developmental process in the interaction of the subject with the temporal environment;

d. whether the mode of perception involved in empathy is the same as that in altruistic defence mechanisms, which raises issues about the misuse of this perception;

e. what are the precise roles of affect and cognition in this mode of perception?

f. what is the relationship to other mental acts such as introspection and countertransference? and

g. what are the roles and function of empathy within theory and clinical practice of psychoanalysis?

In Chapter 3 the notion of empathy is compared to existing psychoanalytic terms. Although it is frequently cited within the literature, empathy is often unclearly articulated in relation to existing terminology. Whereas psychoanalytic descriptions are based on an understanding of psychic processes common to all humans, the phenomenological empathic stance seems to foster an exploration of the uniqueness and difference of the other in a relational setting. This notion of unconcealment differs from psychoanalytic descriptions of empathy, which are aimed at discovering similarities.

In Chapter 4, a reformulation of the concept of empathy is illustrated with the help of clinical examples. This reformulation, I believe, presents a novel hermeneutics of empathy in the context of psychotherapy, and it is offered along with directions for further inquiry, especially for its ramifications in specific clinical work. In proposing mental representation as a basis for empathy, I am suggesting that empathy occurs as a separate mental act within the subject and is episodic in that it allows for the inclusion of objective reality as well as subjective states. As such, empathy can be regarded as a separate category of experience that has epistemological ramifications as well as implications for clinical applications. As an epistemological act, empathy is a means of knowing the other — object, person, event, cultural artefact, and text.

It was this original intentionality that led to the adoption of empathy by aesthetics, an idea that could go back to the eighteenth-century German philosopher, Emmanuel Kant, for whom the a priori forms of intuition (space and time) and categories of understanding (unity/plurality, cause/effect, possibility/impossibility, etc.) combine with sense data to give synthetic knowledge. The experience of the "sublime" suggests the possibility of being a free-standing aesthetic category, and it shares some of the characteristics of empathy. Epistemologically, empathy remains an attempt to define the *noemata* in the horizon of understanding in which other is appropriated in the subjective reality of oneself, i.e. in the process of "double representation".

Furthermore, my contention, as I have argued earlier, is that this process of double representation occurs by means of double representation: a representation of self, be that in the form of memory, experience, part object, imagination or linguistic trace, with a collateral representation of the other. On the basis of congruence, deductions are made about similarities to oneself and on the basis of non-congruence an openness allows for difference. Similarities can be understood on the basis of analogies, to common psychic phenomena, such as defined by principles of psychoanalysis, and differences can be acknowledged by an ontological openness to the unconcealment of the other's self in the present moment.

Thus, the metaphors of psychoanalysis allow for the emergence of understanding on the basis of psychic similarities, and these may include an analysis of transference or an understanding of continuous traits. A phenomenological openness allows for the possibility of difference to emerge and discontinuities in the other's experience.

As it is in the nature of mental acts to be transient, unlike mechanical objects, the appraisal of the other by this means is constantly in a state of flux influenced by other mental acts as well as by changes in the perceiver and the perceived. Thus, as a clinical tool, empathy provides data about longstanding transferential aspects of the other, but also provides traces of the immediate reality of the other. The understanding of the other based on similarities with self is in keeping with the classical Western philosophical notion of self as a discrete, continuous phenomenon.

However, recent trends in Western philosophy attempt at a "deconstruct" of this notion while questioning the continuous nature of self. In discussing the "identity of difference and difference of identity", Mark C. Taylor states that

> philosophy begins and ends with the question of the other. The question is not a question, it is a complex of questions.[1]

Without wishing to enter into a discussion on the philosophical basis of the notion of self, it is perhaps important to locate the problem of empathy within this larger discourse as one question about the larger problem of the means of knowing the other.

Having thus addressed the problem of empathy within a larger discourse of self, it is important to be aware that

---

1 Mark C. Taylor (ed.), *Deconstruction in Context: Literature and Philosophy*, Chicago: Chicago University Press, 1986.

definitions of empathy have been, by and large, unsatisfactory. Psychoanalytic analogies or attempts at understanding the problem of empathy have been beset by problems of semantic and epistemological difficulties. New analogies of this process are provided by developmental studies of the interaction between mother and child, by psychological studies examining the development of empathy and moral reasoning, and by phenomenological explorations of the experience. . . . The future horizons of empathy clearly lies in this direction, although much more work and careful thinking remain to be done in this area before the frontier is likely to open any further.

I trust that my investigation has advanced the field towards that end and brought some needed clarity to an otherwise oblique area.

Bibliography

Agosta, L., "Empathy and Intersubjectivity", in *Empathy I* (ed. Lichtenberg J. et al.), pp. 43-62.

Aristotle, "Rhetorica: Rhetoric", in *The Works of Aristotle*, vol. XI, tr. Robert Rhys, Oxford: The Clarendon Press, 1924. (*The "Art" of Rhetoric*, Loebb Classical Library, Cambridge, MA: Harvard University Press, 1975.)

Basch, M.F., "Empathic Understanding: A Review of the Concept and Some Theoretical Considerations", *Journal of the American Psychoanalytic Association*, **31**: 101-26, 1983.

Beres, D. "The Role of Empathy in Psychotherapy and Psychoanalysis", *Journal of the Hillside Hospital*, **17**: 362-69, 1968.

Beres, D., and J.A. Arlow, "Fantasy and Identification in Empathy", *Psychoanalytic Quarterly*, **43**: 155-81, 1974.

Bergman, A., and A. Wilson, "Thoughts About Stages on the Way to Empathy and the Capacity for Concern", in *Empathy II*, 1984, pp. 59-80.

Berlin, I., *Vico and Herder: Two Studies in the History of Ideas*, New York: Viking, 1976.

Bettis, J.D. (ed.), *Phenomenology of Religion: Eight Modem Descriptions of the Essence of Religion*, New York: Harper & Row, 1969.

Bilimoria, P., "Ethics of Emotions: Some Crosscultural Reflections", in J. Marks and R. Ames (eds.) *Emotions: East & West*, NY: SUNY Press, Spring 1994.

Bion, W.R., "Attacks on Linking", *International Journal of Psychoanalysis*, **40**: 308-15, 1959.

———, "Development of Schizophrenic Thought", *International Journal of Psychoanalysis*, **37**: 344-46, 1953.

———, *Learning from Experience*, London: Maresfield Reprints, 1962.

Birchhead, L.M., "Identification as an Appropriate Component of Therapeutic Growth and Development", *Issues in Mental Health Nursing*, **6**(1-2): 73-88, 1984.

Blomfield, O.H.D., "Group Life and Thinking", Circulated Paper to Training Group of the Aust. Group Psychotherapy Association.

Bromberg, P.M., "Empathy, Anxiety and Reality: A View from the Bridge", *Contemporary Psychoanalysis*, **16**(2): 223-36, 1980.

Brothers, L., "A Biological Perspective on Empathy", *American Journal of Psychiatry*, **146**(1): 10-17, 1989.

Broussard, E.R., "Maternal Empathy: Its Relation to Emerging Self Representations and Empathy in Infants", in *Empathy II* (ed. Lichtenberg, J. et al.), pp. 81-106.

Buber, Martin, *Between Man and Man*, New York: Macmillan, 1965.

Buie, D.H., "Empathy: Its Nature and Limitations", *Journal of the American Psychoanalytic Association*, **29**: 281-307, 1981.

Burlingham, D., "Empathy Between Infant and Mother", *Journal American Psychoanalitic Association*, **15**(4): 764-80, 1964.

Casey, Edward S., *Imaging: A Phenomenological Study*, Bloomington: Indiana University Press, 1979.

Chismar, Douglas, "Empathy and Sympathy: The Important Difference", *The Journal of Value Enquiry*, **22**: 257-66, 1988.

Compton, A., "The Concept of Identification in the Work of Freud, Ferenczi, and Abraham: A Review and Commentary", *Psychoanalytic Quarterly*, **44**: 200-233, 1985.

Condon, W.S., "Communication and Empathy", in *Empathy II*, 1984, pp. 34-58.

Demos, V., "Empathy and Affect: Reflections on Infant Experience", in *Empathy II*, 1984, pp. 9-34.

Deutsch, F., and R.A. Madle, "Empathy: Historic and Current Conceptualizations, Measurement and a Cognitive Theoretical perspective human development", *Human Development*, **18**(4): 267-87, 1975.

Ferenczi, S., "Introjection and Transference" (1909), in E. Jones (ed. and tr.) *First Contributions to Psychoanalysis*, New York: Brunner/Mazel, 1980.

———, "On the Definition of Introjection", in M. Balint (ed.) *Final Contributions to the Problems and Methods of Psychoanalysi*, New York: Basic Books, 1955.

———, "The Elasticity of Psychoanalytic Technique" (1928), in M. Balint (ed.), *Final Contributions to the Problems and Method of Psychoanalysis*, New York: Basic Books, 1955.

———, "The Principle of Relaxation and Neo-Catharsis" (1930), in M. Balint (ed.), *Final Contributions to the Problems and Method of Psychoanalysis*, New York: Brunner/Mazel, 1912; repr. New York: Basic Books, 1955.

Ferenczi, S., and O. Rank, *The Developmental Aims of Psychoanalysis*, USA: Nervous and Mental Disease Publishing Company, 1925.

Fischer, W.J., "On the Phenomenological Approach to Psychology", *Journal of Phenomenological Psychology*, **17**: 65-76, Spring, 1986.

Fliess, R. "Countertransference and Counteridentification", *Journal of the American Psychoanalytic Association*, **1**: 268-84, 1953.

———, "The Metapsychology of the Analyst", *Psychoanalytic Quarterly*, **11**: 211-27, 1942.

Freud, Sigmund, "Group Psychology and the Analysis of the Ego", in *Complete Psychology Works of Sigmund Freud*, ed. and tr. J. Strachey (standard edn.), London: Hogarth Press, 1955, vol. 18: pp. 69-144.

———, *Jokes and Their Relation to the Unconscious (1905)* (standard edn.), London: Hogarth Press, 1960, p. 8.

Gay, Peter, *Freud: A Life for Our Time*, London/New York: Norton, 1988.

Giorgi, A., "Theoretical Justification for the Use of Descriptions in Psychological Research", in P.D. Ashworth, A. Giorgi and A.J.J. Koning (eds.), *Qualitative Research in Psychology: Proceedings of the International Association for Qualitative Research*, Pittsburgh, PA: Dusquesne University Press, 1986.

———, *Phenomenology and Psychological Research*, Pittsburgh, PA: Dusquesne University Press, 1985.

Globus, G.G., "Consciousness and the Brain", *Archives in General Psychiatry*, **29**(2): 167-77, 1973.

Goldstein, A.P., and Y.G Michaels, *Empathy, Development, Training and Consequences*, Hillsdale, NJ: Lawrence Erlbaum, 1985.

Greenson, R., "Empathy and Its Vicissitudes", *International Journal of Psychoanalysis*, **41**: 418-28, 1960.

Grigberg, L., "On a Specific Aspect of Countertransference Due to the Patient's Projective Identification", *International Journal of Psychoanalysis*, **43**: 436-40, 1962.

Grunbaum, Adolf, *The Foundations of Psychoanalysis: A Philosophical Critique*, Berkeley: University of California Press, 1984.

Halasz, G., "Identification: Theoretical and Clinical Aspects", Papers of the Freudian School of Melbourne, ed. Oscar Zentner, 1988.

Harré, Ron (ed.), *The Encyclopaedia Dictionary of Psychology*, Oxford: Basil Blackwell, 1983.

Heimann, P., "On Countertransference", *International Journal of Psychoanalysis*, **31**: 81-84, 1950.

Hume, David, *A Treatise of Human Nature* (1741; 2.1.9-11), rev. edn., Oxford: Clarendon Press, 1978.

———, *Enquiries Concerning Human Understanding and Concerning the Principles of Morals (1978)*, rev. edn., Oxford: Clarendon Press, 1975, p. 189.

Hunsdahl, J.B., "Concerning Einfühlung (Empathy): A Conceptual Analysis of Its Origins and Early Development", *Journal of the History of the Behavioral Sciences*, **3**: 180-91, 1967.

Husserl, Edmund, *Ideas* (tr. W.R. Boyce Gibson), London: Allen and Unwin, 1958.

———, *The Idea of Phenomenology* (tr. W.P. Alston and G. Nakhnika), The Hague: Martinus Nijhoff, 1964.

Jacobs, D., and V. Williams, "Clinical Theory and Scientism: Empathy Research as a Case Study", *Journal of Humanistic Psychology*, **23**(1): 79-96, 1983.

Kainer, R.G.K., "From 'Evenly-Hovering Attention' to Vicarious Introspection: Issues of Listening in Freud and Kohut", *American Journal of Psychoanalysis*, **44**(1): 103-14, Spring 1984.

Kernberg, O.F., "The Treatment of Patients with Borderline Personality Organization", *International Journal of Psychoanalysis*, **49**: 600-19, 1968.

Khan, M.M.R., *The Privacy of the Self*, New York: International University Press, 1974.

Klein, M., "Notes on Some Schizoid Mechanisms", in *Envy and Gratitude and Other Works, 1946-1963*, ed. Seymour Lawrence, New York: Delacorte Press, 1975.

Kohut, Heinz, "Introspection, Empathy and the Semicircle of Mental Health", *International Journal of Psycho-Analysis*, **63**: 395-408, 1982.

———, "Introspection, Empathy, and Psychoanlysis: An Examination of the Relationship Between Mode of Observation and Theory", *Journal of American Psychoanal. Association*, **7**: 459-83, 1959.

Kuhmerker, L., "Learning to Care: The Development of Empathy", *J. Moral Education*, **5**(1): 25-33, 1975.

———, "Social Interaction and the Development of a Sense of Right and Wrong in Young Ren", *J. Moral Education*, **5**(3): 257-64, 1976.

Kuhn, T.S, *The Structure of Scientific Revolution* (rev. edn), Chicago: University of Chicago Press, 1962.

Kultgen, J.H., "Defence of Verstehen", *Personalist*, **53**: 170-87, 1972.

Laplanche, J., and J.B. Pontalis, *The Language of Psychoanalysis*, London: The Hogarth Press and The Institute of Psychoanalysis, 1985.

Lawall, S.N., *Critics of Consciousness: The Existential Structures of Literature*, Cambridge, MA: Harvard University Press, 1968.

Levy, S.T., "Empathy and Psychoanalytic Technique", *Journal of the American Psychoanalytic Association*, **33**: 353-78, 1985.

Lichtenberg, J., M. Bornstein, and D. Silver (eds.), *Empathy I and II* (2 vols), Hillsdale, NJ: The Analytic Press, 1984.

Lichtenberg, J.D., "The Empathic Mode of Perception and Alternative Vantage Points for Psychoanalytic Work", *Psychoanalytic Inquiry*, **1**: 329-55, 1981.

Lipps, Theodor, "Empathy and Aesthetic Pleasure" (tr. Karl Aschenbrenner, 1903), in *Aesthetic Theories: Studies in the Philosophy of Art*, ed. Karl Aschenbrenner and Arnold Isenberg, Englewood Cliff, NJ: Prentice Hall, 1965, pp. 403-12.

———, *Aesthetik*, Hamburg: Voss, 1903.

Lipton, G., and B. Tonge, "The Essence of Mothering Children Under Five", in *Modern Perspective in the Psychiatry of Infancy*, ed. J.G. Howells, New York: Brunner/Mazel, 1979, pp. 191-21.

Little, M., "Countertransferance and the Patient's Response to It", *International Journal of Psychoanalysis*, **32**: 2-40, 1951.

Margulies, A., and L.L. Havens, "The Initial Encounter: What to Do First?", *American Journal of Psychiatry*, **138**(4): 421-28, 1981.

———, "Towards Empathy: The Uses of Wonder", *American Journal of Psychiatry*, **141**(9): 1025-33, 1984.

McDougal, J., "Countertransference and Primitive Communication", in *Plea for a Measure of Insanity*, New York: International Universities Press, 1978.

Meares, Russell, "Keats and the 'Impersonal' Therapist: A Note on Empathy and the Therapeutic Screen", *Psychiatry*, **46**: 73-82, February 1983.

Meissner, W.W., "Notes on Identification, III: The Concept of Identification", *Psychoanalytic Quarterly*, **41**(2): 224-60, 1974.

Merleau-Ponty, M., "The Child's Relations with Others", in *The Sociology of Childhood: Essential Readings*, ed. Jenks C. Batsford, Academic and Educational 1982.

———, *The Phenomenology of Perception* (tr. Colin Smith), London: Routledge, Kegan & Paul, 1962.

Modell, A., "Empathy and the Failure of Empathy", *Bulletin of the Association for Psychoanalytic Medicine*, **18**: 70-75, 1979.

Mohanty, J.N., "Levels of Understanding Intentionality", *The Monist*, **69**(4): 505-20; October, 1986; see also *Phenomenology and Ontology*, The Hague: Martinus Nijhoff, 1970.

———, *The Concept of Intentionality*, Warren Green: St Louis, revised as *Husserl's Concept of Intentionality* (Analecta Husserliana), vol. ID,

Dordrecht: Reidel & Co., 1972, see also Edmund Husserl's *Theory of Meaning*, The Hague: Martinus Hijhoff, 1964.

Mullahy, P., *The Beginnings of Modem American Psychiatry*, Boston: Houghton Mifflin, 1973.

Northrup, G.H., *Psychoanalytic Issues in the Theory of Empathy* (Dissertation), Michigan: University Microfilms International, 1986 (Microfiche).

Ogden, T.H., "On Potential Space", *International Journal of Psychoanalysis*, **66**: 129-41, 1985.

———, "The Concept of Projective Identification", in M. Sandler (ed.), *Projection, Identification and Psychotherapeutic Technique*, New York: International Universities Press, 1987.

Olden, C., "On Adult Empathy with Children", *Psychoanalytic Study of the Child*, **8**: 110-26, 1953.

Olinick, S.L., "A Critique of Empathy and Sympathy", in *Empathy I* (ed. Lichtenberg J. et al.), pp. 137-66.

Ornstein, P.H., "Remarks on the Central Position of Empathy in Psychoanalysis", *Bulletin of the Association for Psychoanalytic Medicine*, **18**: 95-108, 1979.

Parker, Peter, "Is Psychoanalytically Inspired Research Possible for Students of Psychiatry and Clinical Psychology? A flawed option", (unpublished MS).

Poder, M.S., "Projective Identification: An Alternative Hypothesis", *Psychoanalytic Quarterly*, **56**: 431-51, 1987.

Rachman, A., "The Rule of Empathy: Sandor Ferenczi's Pioneering Contributions to the Empathic Method in Psychoanalysis", *American Academy of Psychoanalysis Journal*, **16**(1): 1-27, 1988.

Racker, H., "The Meanings and Uses of Countertransference", *Psychoanalytic Quarterly*, **26**: 303-57, 1957.

Reed, Gail S., "The Antithetical Meaning of the Term 'Empathy' in Psychoanalytic Discourse", in *Empathy I* (ed. Lichtenberg J. et al.), Hillsdale, NJ: The Analytic Press, 1984, pp. 7-24.

Reich, A., "Further Remarks on Countertransference", *International Journal of Psychoanalysis*, **41**: 389-95, 1960.

———, "Empathy and Countertransference", in Annie Reich, *Psychoanalytic Contributions*, New York: International Universities Press, 1966.

———, "On Countertransference", *International Journal of Psychoanalysis*, **32**: 25-31, 1951.

Reik, T., *Listening with the Third Ear*, New York: E. Farrar Strauss, 1937.

Roazen, P., *Freud and His Followers*, New York: New York University Press, 1984.

Rycroft, Charles, "Symbolism and Its Relationship to the Primary and Secondary Processes", *International Journal of Psychoanalysis*, **37**, 2-3, 1956.

Sandler, J., C. Dare and A. Holder, *The Patient and the Analyst*, London: Maresfield Library, 1973.

Sartre, Jean-Paul, "Intentionality: A Fundamental Feature of Husserl's Phenomenology" (tr. J. Fell), *Journal of the British Society for Phenomenology*, **I**: 4-5, 1970.

Schafer, R., "Generative Empathy in the Treatment Situation", *Psychoanalytic Quarterly*, **28**: 342-73, 1959.

Schafer, Roy, "Discussion", in *Empathy I* (ed. Lichtenberg J. et al.), pp. 31-36.

Scheler, Max, *The Nature of Sympathy*, tr. Peter Heath, Hamden, CI: Archon Books, 1954.

Schwaber, E., "Discussion", in *Empathy I* (ed. Lichtenberg J. et al.), pp. 25-30.

Searles, H.F., "The Self in the Countertransference", *Issues in Ego Psychology*, **2**(2): 49-56, 1979.

Shapiro, T., "Empathy: A Critical Re-evaluation", in *Empathy" I* (ed. Lichtenberg J. et al.), pp. 103-28.

———, "The Development and Distortions of Empathy", *Psychoanalytic Quarter*ly, **43**(1)4-25, 1974.

Sharma, Renuka M., "Empathy: A Retrospective on Its Development in Psychotherapy", *Australian and New Zealand Journal of Psychiatry*, **26**(3): 377-90, 1993.

Silver, D., "Introductory Remarks: Developmental Aspects of Empathy", in Lichtenberg et al. (eds.), *Empathy II*, 1985, pp. 3-8.

Solomon, Robert C., *The Passions*, NY: Doubleday/Anchor, 1977.

Spence Jr, J.H., "Discussion", in *Empathy I* (ed. Lichtenberg J. et al.), pp. 37-42.

Spiegelberg, Herbert, *Phenomenology in Psychology and Psychiatry: A Historical Introduction*, Evanston: Northwestern University Press, 1972.

Stein, Edith, *On the Problem of Empathy*, tr. W. Stein, The Hague: Martinus Nijhoff, 1964.

Stern, D., *The Interpersonal World of the Infant: A View from Psychoanalysis and Developmental Psychology*, New York: Basic Books, 1985.

Stolorow, R.D., and G.E. Atwood, "The Work of Stolorow and Atwood" Symposium Psychoanalytic Phenomenology (reply to R. White, M. Basch and M. Nissam Sabat), **73**(3): 301-08, 1986.

Sullivan, H.S., "Personal Psychopathology", William Alanson White Psychiatric Foundation, Washington DC (unpublished MS), 1965 (quoted in Mullahy, 1973).

———, "Socio-Psychiatric Research", *American Journal of Psychiatry*, **10**: 977-91, 1931.

———, *The Interpersonal Theory of Psychiatry*, ed H.S. Perry and Gawel, New York: Norton, 1953.

Tansey, M.J., and W.F.H. Burke, *Understanding Countertransference from Projective Identification to Empathy*, Hillsdale, NJ: The Analytic Press, 1989.

Tatarkiewicz, W., and M. Golebiowski, "Aesthetic Experience: The Early History of the Concept" *Dialectics and Humanism*, Autumn 1973, pp. 19-30.

Taylor, Mark C. (ed.), *Deconstruction in Context: Literature and Philosophy*, Chicago: Chicago University Press, 1986.

Titchener, E.B., *Lectures on the Experimental Psychology of the Thought Processes*, New York: Macmillan, 1909.

Truax, C.B., and K.M. Mitchell, "Research on Certain Therapist Interpersonal Skills in Relation to Process and Outcome", in A.E. Bergin and S.L. Garfield (eds.) *Handbook of Psychotherapy and Behavior Change: An Empirical Analysis*, New York: Wiley, 1971.

Tyson, R.L., "Countertransference Evolution in Theory and practice", *Journal of the American Psychoanalytic Association*, **34**(2): 251-74, 1986.

Wallerstein, R.S., "Self-Psychology and Classical Psychoanalytic Psychology: The Nature of Their Relationship", *Psychoanalysis and Contemporary Thought*, **6**: 4, 1983.

Wertz, F.J., "From Everyday to Psychological Description: Analysing the Moments of a Qualitative Data Analysis", in *Journal of Phenomenological Psychology*, **14**(2): 197-241, 1983 Fall.

Winnicott, D.W., "Hate in the Countertransference", *International Journal of Psychoanalysis*, **30**: 69-74, 1949.

———, "The Capacity to Be Alone", *International Journal of Psychoanalysis*, **39**: 416-20, 1958.

———, "The Location of Cultural Experience", *International Journal of Psychoanalysis*, **48**: 368, 1967.

———, "The Theory of the Parent-Infant Relationship", in D.W. Winnicott ed. *The Maturational Process and the Facilitating Environment*, New York: International Universities Press, 1965.

———, "Transitional Objects and Transitional Phenomena", *International Journal of Psychoanalysis*, **34**: 89-97, 1953.

Index